ENTERPRISE 1

COURSEBOOK

Beginner

Virginia Evans - Jenny Dooley

Express Publishing

Contents

MODULE 1 · MODULE 2 · MODULE 3 · MODULE 4

LISTENING & SPEAKING	COMMUNICATION	WRITING
asking for personal information; talking about landmarks; Pronunciation — names of countries and capitals	introducing people	Project — famous landmarks; introducing ourselves and other people
radio programme about missing people; describing people; spelling; Pronunciation — /iː/, /ı/	greetings; saying goodbye	Project — descriptions of people; an Internet advertisement for a pen-friend
describing a house/flat; talking to an estate agent; Pronunciation — /ɑː/, /æ/	asking for and giving addresses and phone numbers	Project — letter to a friend describing your house and room; advertisements for a house/flat to rent
days you like/hate; talking about a person; Pronunciation — /s/, /z/, /ız/	identifying people	Project — family tree; a letter to a pen-friend
daily routine; interviewing a celebrity; Pronunciation — /θ/, /ð/	telling the time	Project — opening hours in your country; article about a celebrity's daily routine
identifying animals through sounds; describing animals; quiz about animals; Pronunciation — /ɛ/, /ɜː/	asking about pets	Project — descriptions of animals; facts about animals
identifying actions through sounds; fashion show — describing clothes, making comments on clothes; Pronunciation — /n/, /ŋ/	buying clothes	Project — different seasons in your country; a postcard to a friend
offering; ordering food at a restaurant/ fast food restaurant; Pronunciation — /s/, /z/, /ız/	ordering food; accepting/refusing offers	Project — article about eating habits in Britain; advertisement for a restaurant
talking about changes in a place; talking about past abilities; Pronunciation — /s/, /ʃ/	giving directions; asking for information	Project — what you were like at the age of seven; a "then-and-now" article
painters and paintings/composers and music; Vivaldi's life; Pronunciation — /t/, /d/, /ıd/	asking personal questions about the recent past	Project — biography of Mozart; biography of Vivaldi
sequence of events; telling a story; Pronunciation — /ʌ/, /ɒ/	reporting emergencies	Project — beginning/ending for a story; a story about a fire
geography quiz; deciding on a hotel; Pronunciation — /tʃ/, /dʒ/	making comments; making suggestions	Project — description of your town; article describing Antwerp
tomorrow's weather forecast; asking for personal information; Pronunciation — /h/ pronounced or silent	accepting/refusing invitations	Project — next week's horoscopes; letter to a friend about your future plans
advice about healthy living; house rules, school rules; Pronunciation — /r/ pronounced or silent	giving advice; giving/refusing permission; expressing obligation/prohibition	Project — letter giving advice; leaflet giving advice to people at the beach
telephone conversation; meeting a friend abroad; identifying correct responses; Pronunciation — /ʃ/, /tʃ/	making a reservation; inviting sb out; buying souvenirs	Project — letter to a friend; letter to a friend from a holiday destination reporting your experiences

Published by Express Publishing

Liberty House, New Greenham Park, Newbury, Berkshire RG19 6HW
Tel.: (0044) 1635 817 363 Fax: (0044) 1635 817 463
e-mail: inquiries@expresspublishing.co.uk
http://www.expresspublishing.co.uk

© Virginia Evans - Jenny Dooley, 1998

Design and Illustration © Express Publishing, 1998

First published 1998
New edition 2002

ISBN 1-84216-089-3

Acknowledgements.

Authors' Acknowledgements

We would like to thank all the staff at Express Publishing who have contributed their skills to producing this book. Thanks are due in particular to:
Mary Palmer (Editor in Chief), Peter Harris and Anna Miller (senior editors), Ann Doyle and Sheila Howard (editorial assistants), Philippa Porter
(senior production controller), and the Express Publishing design team, Tony Boyle (recording producer) and Debbie Ellis, Julie Brown, Douglas
Stephens, Tamzin Thompson, Diana Thomson, Elaine Emery, Ann Mitchell, Helen Smith, Tasso Dirlis and Steve Mason for their support and
patience. We would also like to thank those institutions and teachers who piloted the manuscript, and whose comments and feedback were invaluable in the production of the book.

The authors and publishers wish to thank the following who have kindly given permission for the use of copyright material:

Woman's Own magazine for the article "We were trapped by fire ... in a lion's den" by Rupert Halden (on p. 77); picture of "Queen of May" (on p. 163)
© Phil Gee 1997 www.hayfield.uk.net

Colour Illustrations: Terry Wilson

**While every effort has been made to trace all the copyright holders, if any have been inadvertently overlooked the publishers will be pleased to
make the necessary arrangements at the first opportunity.**

Introduction

Enterprise 1 Beginner is a complete course for students studying English at beginner level. It provides them with extensive, systematic and well-integrated practice in the productive and receptive skills necessary for successful communication in both oral and written forms of the language.

The course embodies a multi-syllabus approach and a wide variety of presentation methodology. Traditional emphasis on systematic learning of grammar and vocabulary is balanced with practice in communicative language use, the methodical development of linguistic sub-skills, and attention to details of spelling and pronunciation. Graded, structured material which facilitates learning is balanced with more authentic, unsimplified material which encourages language acquisition. Controlled practice leads from the initial learning of language items to genuinely communicative and creative activities.

The course consists of fifteen units in four modules and a variety of supplementary material, including a workbook. In total, *Enterprise 1 Beginner* may be covered in 70-75 teaching hours.

Each unit ensures coverage of a core of common, useful language related to topics of general interest with which students need to be familiar. The units follow the same basic structure, outlined below:

- **Lead-in sections** draw on the students' knowledge of the given topic while previewing the new items of vocabulary and grammar to be learnt in the unit. The section ends with a listening activity, requiring students to listen to a recording of the reading text and complete a task, such as checking information, multiple matching and so on. This prepares students for the reading text which follows, by familiarising them with the gist of the passage.

- **Reading sections** consist of 50- to 150-word texts on factual topics, reflecting authentic types and styles of writing. These texts allow students to develop sub-skills such as reading for gist or for specific information, and present new vocabulary in a meaningful context.

- **Language Development sections** formally present new vocabulary and grammar items, and practise them in a stimulating and balanced variety of tasks. These include listening and speaking activities to ensure the integrated development of skills, and incorporate the teaching of notions such as sequence, purpose and so on.
  - **Vocabulary sections** practise and extend the vocabulary introduced in the reading text, through various types of exercises. A particular feature of the book is the teaching of collocations, helping students to remember vocabulary items as parts of set expressions.
  - **Grammar sections** present grammar items clearly and concisely, and reinforce students' understanding of these through grammar exercises. A range of activities then provide controlled practice leading to free use of the grammar items in genuine language tasks.

- **Reading and Listening sections** deal with meaningful texts on authentic, cross-cultural topics. These texts exploit the intrinsic interest of the subject matter as well as providing relatively unsimplified language to cater for language acquisition. The listening tasks improve students' listening skills while preparing them for the reading tasks, which involve such skills as scanning for information, selecting relevant sections of texts and so on.

- **Pronunciation** activities help students to recognise sounds and reproduce them correctly. Intonation is regularly modelled and practised in numerous dialogues throughout each unit. All pronunciation exercises are on the cassettes accompanying the coursebook.

- **Communication sections** provide varied practice involving meaningful exchanges which resemble real-life communication, and include language functions (i.e. offering, suggesting, etc.), the standard expressions associated with communicative situations (i.e. ordering a meal, travel arrangements, etc.), and sociolinguistic features such as the polite expressions appropriate to "friendly" or formal social contexts.

- **Writing sections** provide more extensive practice and consolidation of new language items. Writing tasks are thoroughly prepared beforehand, following guided practice of the language to be used, and based on the model provided by the initial reading text. Additionally, a listening activity ingeniously provides the information and plan to be followed, ensuring systematic, controlled development of writing skills. All writing activities are based on realistic types and styles of writing task, such as letters, descriptions, stories, articles and so on.

- **Module Self-Assessment sections** after every fourth unit reinforce the students' understanding of the topics, vocabulary and structures presented in the previous units. The material has been designed to help students learn new language in the context of what they have already mastered, rather than in isolation.

- **Three entertaining adventure stories** in a 'comic strip' format, presented in two episodes each, invite students to read for enjoyment and provide invaluable consolidation by means of an alternative approach.

- **Culture Clips**

  The coursebook is accompanied by:
  a) an easy-to-use **Teacher's Book** with full answers to the exercises in the Student's Book, useful suggestions for presenting and conducting the exercises, and four tests (each in two different versions);
  b) **Class audio cassettes** or **audio CDs** containing all listening activities, and **Student's audio cassettes** or **audio CDs**;
  c) **Enterprise Beginner Workbook** in which students can revise, consolidate and extend their language learning through a variety of engaging tasks.
  d) **Enterprise Beginner Test Booklet** containing nine write-in tests, a Mid-term test and an Exit test, which aim to assess students' progress throughout the course.

People & Homes ....

◄ Read, listen, talk and write about...

Hi!

Unit 1
- people; countries; nationalities; landmarks
- jobs

A Friend in Need!

Unit 2
- people's facial features
- colours
- abilities

Module 1

Units 1 - 4

Home, Sweet Home!

Unit 3

◀ **Learn how to ...**

- introduce people
- greet; say goodbye
- ask for and give adresses & phone numbers
- identify people

◀ **Practise ...**

- a-an/plurals
- to be/have (got)/can
- this/these - that/those
- there is/there are
- possessive adjectives/ pronouns
- possessive case
- prepositions of place
- present simple

- houses around the world & their special features
- furniture & appliances

Like Father, Like Son!

Unit 4

- families & relationships
- likes & dislikes

Hi!

A □□
They are ....

Lead-in

1 Look at the pictures. Which people are from:
Spain, India, Scotland or Brazil?

2 ▭ **a) Listen and repeat.**

I am from Edinburgh, Scotland.
I'm forty years old.
I'm not married.
They're friends and they're from Brazil.
I'm a student at an English boarding-school.
My favourite sport is golf.
Where is he from?
What's his job?
How old is he?

b) Can you explain what the sentences above mean?

3 ▭ **Listen and match the letters to the numbers you hear.**

B □
I'm a ....

C □□
They are ....

D □□
I'm a ....

Reading

4 Read the texts and label the pictures with the correct word in bold. Then, answer the questions.

a) Where is Fergus from? What's his job?
b) How old is Diego? What's his favourite sport?
c) Where are Carlos and Rosa from? How old is Carlos? How old is Rosa?
d) Where is Veena from? What's her favourite sport?

1 Hello! I'm Fergus and I'm from Edinburgh, Scotland. I'm forty years old. I'm a **musician**. I'm not married. My favourite sport is golf.

2 This is Diego and this is Marco. They're friends and they're from Brazil. Diego is thirty-five years old and Marco is twenty-seven years old. They are **farmers**. Diego's favourite sport is football and Marco's favourite sport is basketball.

3 This is Carlos and this is Rosa. They're friends and they're from Spain. Carlos is twenty-two years old and Rosa is twenty years old. They are **dancers**. His favourite sport is football and her favourite sport is tennis.

4 Hi there! I'm Veena from New Delhi. It's in India. I'm twelve years old and I'm a **student** at an English boarding-school in Manchester. My favourite sport is volleyball.

• Speaking

a) Look at the short texts, then ask and answer questions, as in the example.

*S1: **Where's** Fergus **from**?*
S2: He's from Edinburgh, Scotland.
   ***How old is** he and **what's** his **job**?*
S3: He's forty and he's a musician.
   ***What's** his **favourite sport**?*
S4: His favourite sport is golf.

b) Read the texts. Copy and complete the table. Look at your notes and talk about each person, as in the example.

	Origin	Age	Job	Favourite Sport
Fergus	*Edinburgh, Scotland*	*forty*	*musician*	*golf*
Diego	Brazil	35	farmer	fooball
Marco	Brazil	27	farmer	basketball
Carlos	Spain	22	dancer	foot Ball
Rosa	Spain	20	dancer	Tennis
Veena	New Delhi	12	student	Vollyball

Fergus is from Edinburgh, Scotland. He's forty years old and he's a musician. His favourite sport is golf.

Language Development

• Vocabulary

5 🔊 **Match the cardinal numbers to the ordinal numbers, then listen and check. Listen again and repeat.**

(1) one — second (2nd)
(2) two — fourth (4th)
(3) three — sixth (6th)
(4) four — first (1st)
(5) five — third (3rd)
(6) six — fifth (5th)

(7) seven — eleventh (11th)
(8) eight — ninth (9th)
(9) nine — twelfth (12th)
(10) ten — seventh (7th)
(11) eleven — eighth (8th)
(12) twelve — tenth (10th)

6 🔊 **Write the numbers, then listen and repeat.**

thirteen .13. | fifteen .15. | seventeen .17. | nineteen .19.
fourteen .14. | sixteen .16. | eighteen .18. | twenty .20.

7 🔊 **Write the missing numbers as words, then listen and repeat.**

20 twenty	69 *Sixty nine*
21 ...*twenty-one*...	70 seventy
30 thirty	76 *Seventy six*
34 *Thirty four*	80 eighty
40 forty	87 *eighty seven*
45 *forty five*	90 ninety
50 fifty	98 *ninety eight*
52 *fifty two*	**100 one hundred**
60 sixty	**200 two hundred**

8 **Fill in the gaps with words from the list, then make sentences, as in the example.**

Brazil, Mexico City, Argentina, Japanese, Greek, Spain, Finland, American, Canada, Turkey

Paolo is Brazilian. He's from Brasilia, Brazil.

Name	Nationality	Capital	Country
Paolo	Brazilian	Brasilia	*Brazil*
Pablo	Spanish	Madrid	Spain
Jason	Canadian	Ottawa	Ottawa
Ito	Tokyo	Tokyo	Japan
Thomas	Argentinian	Buenos Aires	Buenos Aires
Mike	USA	Washington DC	the USA
Costas	Greece	Athens	Greece
Hans	Finnish	Helsinki	Finnish
Rico	Mexican	Mexico	Mexico
Ali	Turkish	Ankara	Ankara

9 **Look at the pictures and fill in the capital of each country. Then, ask and answer questions, as in the example.**

Moscow, Cairo, Warsaw, Rome, Budapest, Beijing, Paris

*S1: **Where** is Cairo?*
*S2: **In** Egypt. **It's the capital of** Egypt.*

1 Egypt
Cairo

2 France
Paris

3 Italy
Roma

4 Poland
Poland

5 Hungary
....

6 Russia
Moscu

7 China
China

• **Grammar:** The verb "to be" (present simple)

Affirmative		Negative	
Full form	**Short form**	**Full form**	**Short form**
I am	I'm	I am not	I'm not
you are	you're	you are not	you aren't
he is	he's	he is not	he isn't
she is	she's	she is not	she isn't
it is	it's	it is not	it isn't
we are	we're	we are not	we aren't
you are	you're	you are not	you aren't
they are	they're	they are not	they aren't

Interrogative	Short Answers
Am I ...?	Yes, I am. / No, I'm not.
Are you ...?	Yes, you are. / No, you aren't.
Is he ...?	Yes, he is. / No, he isn't.
Is she ...?	Yes, she is. / No, she isn't.
Is it ...?	Yes, it is. / No, it isn't.
Are we ...?	Yes, we are. / No, we aren't.
Are you ...?	Yes, you are. / No, you aren't.
Are they ...?	Yes, they are. / No, they aren't.

Are you from Spain? No, I'm not.

10 **Fill in 'm, 's, 're, 'm not, isn't or aren't.**

1 She isn't from Spain. She ...'s... from Mexico.
2 You ..aren't........ Hungarian. You are Italian.
3 My favourite sport is tennis. It ..isn't.. football.
4 I am British. I ..'m not.. French.
5 We aren't musicians. We ..are..... students.
6 I ..am...... a musician. I'm not a teacher.
7 Tony's sixteen years old. He .....is....... sixty years old.
8 They aren't from Egypt. They ..are...... from Brazil.

11 **Fill in: is, are, 's, 're, 'm, aren't or isn't.**

1 A: ...*Is*... he from Mexico?
   B: No, he ..isn't. He ....'s..... from Japan.
2 A: ....are.... they Spanish?
   B: No, they ..aren't. . They ....are.... Canadian.
3 A: What ....'s......... your favourite sport?
   B: My favourite sport ......is......... tennis.
4 A: ......is........ she twenty years old?
   B: No, she ..isn't. She ....is....... twenty-two.
5 A: ......'s...... Stella from Hungary?
   B: Yes, she ..is.. . She ....'s..... from Budapest.
6 A: How old ....are..... you?
   B: I ....am.... twenty-three.

the Taj Mahal (Agra)

the Pyramids
(Cairo)

the Eiffel
Tower
(Paris)

Big Ben
(London)

the Parthenon
(Athens)

the White House
(Washington DC)

St Basil's
Cathedral
(Moscow)

the Sydney Opera House
(Sydney)

the Statue of Liberty
(New York)

Pronunciation

12 🔊 **Listen and repeat.**

*Australia, New Delhi, Edinburgh, Egypt, Hungary,
Moscow, Beijing, Russia, Turkey, Warsaw*

• Game

13 **You are the leader. Pretend you are from one of
the countries in the list below. Write it on a piece
of paper. The other students try to guess which
country you are from by asking questions, as in
the example. The student who guesses correctly
goes next.**

*Britain, India, Russia, France, Germany, Holland,
Turkey, Brazil, Italy, Poland, Egypt, Australia*

| S1: *Are you from Italy?* | S2: *Are you from Egypt?* |
| L: *No, I'm not.* | L: *Yes, I am.* |

• Speaking

14 **Look at the pictures. Ask and answer questions,
as in the example.**

the Pyramids – Brazil?
the Taj Mahal – India?
Big Ben – England?
the Eiffel Tower – Italy?
the Parthenon – Poland?
the White House – the USA?
St Basil's Cathedral – Hungary?
the Sydney Opera House – Canada?
the Statue of Liberty – the USA?

S1: *Are the Pyramids in Brazil?*
S2: *No, they aren't. They're in Egypt. Is the
Taj-Mahal in India?*
S3: *Yes, it is. Is ...*

Writing (Project)

**Use the pictures from the Photo File section and
write sentences, as in the example.**

The Pyramids are in Cairo, Egypt.

• Grammar: the indefinite article a/an

---

a - an

We use **a/an** before singular nouns. *a dancer, an actor*
We use **a** before consonant sounds (b, c, d, f, etc).
*He's **a** teacher.*
We use **an** before vowel sounds (a,e,i,o,u).
*She's **an** actress.*

---

15 Add *a* or *an* to the words in the list, then label the pictures. Finally, in pairs, ask and answer questions, as in the example.

artist, astronaut, doctor, engineer, pilot, postman, vet, waiter

SA: **What's** his name?   SB: Twenty-seven.
SB: *Steven.*   SA: **What's** his **job?**
SA: **How old is** he?   SB: *He's **a** waiter.*

Steven (27) — 1 .....a waiter.....
Mark (38)
Bill (45) — 2 *an astronaut*
Ted (39) — 3 ....
Helen (42) — 4 *a Dr.*
Tim (29)
5 *an vet*
Paul (60)
6 *an artist*
7 *an eng...*
John (30) — 8 *a postman*

16 📻 Read the dialogue, then listen and fill in the missing words. In pairs, read out the dialogue.

A: Nice party, isn't it?
S: Yes, it's great.
A: I'm Alison, by the way. 1) *What's* your name?
S: I'm Steve, Steve Blair. Nice to meet you.
A: Nice to meet you, too. 2) *Where* are you from?
S: I'm from Scotland.
A: Where exactly?
S: Glasgow. What about you?
A: I'm from Birmingham. 3) *What's* your job?
S: I'm a doctor. And you?
A: I'm a student.
S: Really? 4) *How* old are you?
A: I'm twenty-one. And you?
S: Well, I'm thirty-five.
A: Thirty-five! Are you really?
S: Yeah!!!

17 📼 a) Listen to the dialogue and repeat it. In pairs, use your names to act out similar dialogues.

Tony: Excuse me. Are you **Rita Brian**?
Rita: Yes, I am.
Tony: Hi. I'm your new neighbour, **Tony, Tony Brown**.
Rita: Oh, hello, **Tony**. Nice to meet you.
Tony: Nice to meet you, too.

📼 b) Listen to this dialogue and put it into the correct order.

1 ☐ **Jane:** Hello, Patrick. Patrick, this is Lucy. She's my friend from America.
4 ☐ **Lucy:** Pleased to meet you, too.
3 ☐ **Patrick:** Hi, Jane.
2 ☐ **Patrick:** Pleased to meet you, Lucy.

- ## Communication: Introducing People

18 📟 **Write the sentences in the correct speech bubbles, then listen and check. Finally, act out the dialogues.**

- *Pleased to meet you.*
- *Pleased to meet you, too.*
- *Mr Potter, this is Mr Jackson.*
- *I'm Gillian Jones, but please call me Gill.*
- *Hello! I'm Frank Smith. What's your name?*

- ## Vocabulary Revision Game

19 **Work in two teams. Take it in turns to choose words from the list and make sentences. Each correct sentence gets one point. The team with the most points is the winner.**

musician, years old, name, favourite, pleased, neighbour, capital, married, farmers, where, job

Team A S1: Fergus is a musician.

20 📟 **Listen and fill in the missing information, then talk about some of the teachers who work at Mortimer College, as in the example.**

Hello!
I'm Rashid Al Hibb. I'm from Alexandria, Egypt. I'm sixteen years old and I'm a student at Mortimer College.

Mary Stuart
Dublin, Ireland
.....*30*..... years old
English teacher

John Parry
Glasgow, Scotland
.....*40*.... years old
Maths teacher

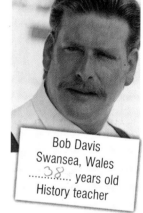

Bob Davis
Swansea, Wales
.....*38*... years old
History teacher

This is Mary Stuart. She's from Dublin, Ireland. She's thirty years old and she's an English teacher at Mortimer College.

Writing

You are a foreign student at Mortimer College . You are responsible for the college magazine and this is the first page of the first issue. Introduce yourself to the readers. Start with: *Hello! I'm* ... **. Then, introduce some of the teachers who work at the college. Start with:** *This is* ... *. He/She is* ... **. Use the information from Ex. 20 and the pictures from the Photo File section, as well as a picture of yourself.**

Words of Wisdom

Read this sentence. What does it mean?

- A stranger is a friend you haven't met yet.

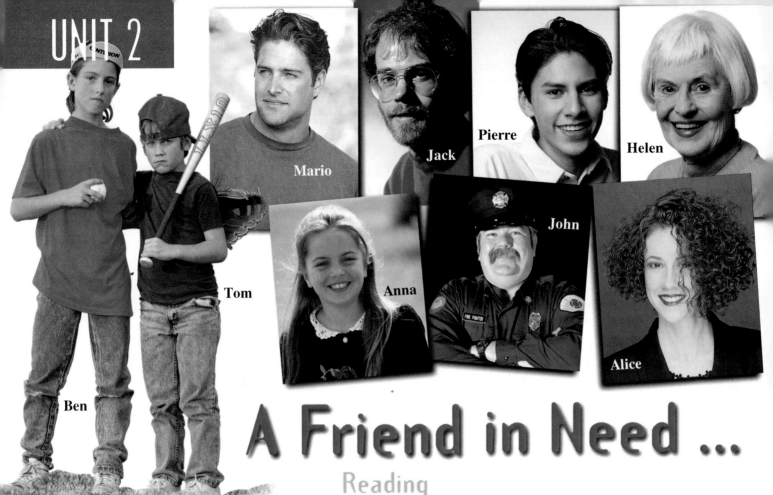

UNIT 2

Lead-in

1 Look at the pictures. Who's got ...

brown, curly hair? brown, wavy hair? short grey hair? long straight fair hair? dark hair? a moustache? a beard and a moustache?

2 Fill in the names of the people in the pictures.

1 ....~~Pierre 17 year~~.... is old.
2 ....~~Pierre~~.... is quite tall and slim.
3 ....~~He~~.... is short and quite slim.
4 ....~~He~~.... is middle-aged and Pierre is young.
5 .... is well-built.
6 .... is fat.

3 📼 Read the sentences, then listen and match the sentences to the speakers.

Speakers

1 "I love playing computer games."
2 "I like playing the guitar."
3 "I like skiing."
4 "Hope to hear from you soon."

| Mario |
| Pierre |
| Anna |

A Friend in Need ...

Reading

4 Read the Internet advertisements for pen-friends and answer the questions. Then, explain the words in bold.

1 What can Pierre do?
2 How old is Mario?
3 Who has got brown eyes?
4 Who is tall and well-built?
5 Is Mario's hair curly?
6 What can Anna do?
7 What is the last sentence in each advertisement?

1

Hello. My name's Pierre and I'm seventeen years old. **I live in** Paris, France. I have got short straight dark hair and **brown eyes**. I'm **quite tall** and **slim**. **I love playing computer games and** I can play tennis **very well**. I like reading too. Please **e-mail me** today!

2

Hi! My name is Anna and I am eleven years old. I live in Moscow, Russia. I have got long straight fair hair and **green eyes**. I'm quite **short** and I like skiing. I can **play the piano** quite well. Please be my e–mail **pen pal**.

3

Hi! My name's Mario and I'm twenty-six years old. I live in Florence, Italy. I'm tall and well-built with brown, wavy hair and brown eyes. I like playing the **guitar** and I love **dancing**. I can speak French too. **Hope to hear** from you soon.

12

• Speaking

Read the advertisements again. Copy the table below and complete it. Then, look at your notes and talk about the people, as in the example.

	Pierre	Anna	Mario
Age:	17	*Pierre*	*Pierre*
Lives in:	Paris, France	*Pierre*	*Pierre*
Hair:	short straight dark	*Pierre*	*Pierre*
Eyes:	brown	*Pierre*	*Pierre*
Height:	quite tall	*Pierre*	*Pierre*
Build:	slim	*Pierre*	*Pierre*
Likes/ Loves:	playing computer games, reading	*Pierre*	*Pierre*
Can:	play tennis very well	*Pierre*	*Pierre*

Pierre is seventeen years old. He lives in Paris, France. He has got short straight dark hair and brown eyes. He is quite tall and slim. He likes playing computer games and reading. He can play tennis very well.

Language Development

• Vocabulary

5 Label the different parts of the face, then point to them on your face and name them.

cheek, chin, ear, eye, hair, mouth, nose, teeth, lips

1 ....hair...........
9 .....*ear*.....
2 .....*eye*.....
3 .....*nose*.....
8 .....*cheek*.....
4 .....*teeth*.....
7 .....*mouth*.....
5 .....*lips*.....
6 .....*chin*.....

6 Use the words in the list to write the opposites of the phrases below.

small, short, fair, thin, curly, fat

1 tall boy ≠ *short boy*
2 slim girl ≠ .....*fat*.....
3 long hair ≠ .....*short*.....
4 straight hair ≠ *curly*
5 dark hair ≠ .....*fair*.....
6 full lips ≠ .....*thin*.....
7 big nose ≠ .....*small*.....
8 big eyes ≠ .....*small*.....

Now use some of these phrases to describe your partner.

*Ted is **tall** and **slim**. He's got **short dark hair** and **thin lips**. He's got ...*

7 Label the colours.
green, blue, black, red, brown, grey
Which of these adjectives are often used to describe: a) hair? b) eyes? c) both?

1 ...red... 2 *Black* 3 *Green*
4 *Grey* 5 *Blue* 6 *Brown*

Brown

• Grammar: have got ('ve got) has got ('s got)

Affirmative	Negative
I/you/we/they**'ve got** he/she/it**'s got**	I/you/we/they **haven't got** he/she/it **hasn't got**

Interrogative and Short Answers:

Have I/you/we/they **got** ...? — **Yes,** I/you/we/they **have. No,** I/you/we/they **haven't.**

Has he/she/it **got** ...? — **Yes,** he/she/it **has. No,** he/she/ it **hasn't.**

We use **have got/has got** to express possession. ***I've got** a dog. My dog **has got** long ears.*

8 Read the advertisements in Ex. 4 again and complete the sentences using: *have, haven't, has* **or** *hasn't.*

1 ...Has... Pierre got a beard? No, he *hasn't*.
2 *Have* Mario and Pierre got brown eyes? *Yes, they have*
3 *Has* Anna got long hair? *Yes, she has*
4 *Have* Mario got a beard? *No, he hasn't*
5 Anna *has* got brown hair.
6 *Has* Mario and Pierre got fair hair? *Yes, they have*

9 *The pictures show people from the Wessex area who are missing.* **Look at their pictures and describe them.** 📟 **Listen and label them with their names from the list.**

Chris, Sally, Jim, Peter, Mary

1 *Sally*

2 *Chris*

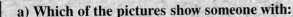

3 *Jim* 4 *Mary* 5 *Peter*

• Game

10 **Choose one of the people in Ex. 9 and describe him or her to your classmates. The student who guesses correctly chooses another person and the game continues. Use these words:**

young, middle-aged, curly, long, straight, slim, well-built, beard, moustache, big nose

• Reading & Listening

11 **a) Which of the pictures show someone with:**
 1 a pale complexion? – *(D)*
 2 light brown skin? *(C)*
 3 very dark skin and a wide, flattish nose? *(E)*
 4 dark slanting eyes and a yellowish complexion? *(A)*
 5 dark brown eyes and dark skin? *B*
b) 📟 **Listen and match the numbers to the pictures.**
 c) Read the texts and answer the questions.
 d) Read the texts again and explain the words in bold.

1 People from countries such as Denmark, Norway and Sweden are usually tall with fair hair, blue eyes and a **pale complexion**. *(3)*

2 Most people in **Mediterranean countries,** such as Italy, Spain and Greece, are rather short. They have usually got black or dark brown hair, brown eyes and **light brown skin**. *(1)*

3 Most people from **central** and **southern** parts of Africa have got black curly hair and very **dark skin**. They have also got dark brown eyes, full lips and a **wide, flattish** nose. *(4)*

4 People from Arab countries such as Saudi Arabia, Iraq and Libya have usually got dark hair and dark brown eyes. They have also got **dark skin**. *(6)*

5 The northern Chinese are quite short, with thick black hair and dark, **slanting eyes**. They have got a small nose and a yellowish complexion.

Questions

1 What do people from these areas look like?
 • Denmark, Norway and Sweden
 • Mediterranean countries
 • central and southern parts of Africa
 • Arab countries
 • northern China
2 What do people from your country look like? *most People from my country Look like dark Complexion, Black Hair*

A

C

B

D   E

He always says Get out when I'm on the bus, something bloody...

Writing (Project)

Use the pictures from the Photo File section and write descriptions of the people. Write about their *age, hair, eyes, height* and *build*.

● Grammar: can

!

Affirmative:
I/you/he/she/it/we/they **can** run.

Negative:
I/you/he/she/it/we/they **can't** run.

Interrogative:
Can I/you/he/she/it/we/they run?

Short answers:
Yes, I/you/he/she/it/we/they **can**.
No, I/you/he/she/it/we/they **can't**.

Can is the same in all persons. We use **can + the base form of a verb** to express **ability** or a **polite request**.
Tom can play football. (ability)
Can you help me, please? (polite request)

● Can (expressing ability)

12 a) Look at the pictures and the list of words below. Ask and answer questions, as in the example.

guitar, car, train, piano, bus, dog, cat, computer, helicopter, motorbike, plane
S1: *Can you see a guitar?*
S2: *No, I can't. Can you see a car?*
S3: *Yes, I can. etc.*

b) Look at the pictures in Ex. 12 again and listen to the sounds. First tick (✓), then say what you *can* or *can't hear.*

*I **can hear** a cat, **but I can't hear** a motorbike.*

13 Match the phrases in the list to the pictures. Then, in pairs, ask and answer questions to find out what your partner *can* or *can't* do, as in the example.

a. cook well b. dance well c. speak English well d. run fast
e. walk fast f. read fast g. swim fast h. type fast

S1: *Can you cook?* 7
S2: *Yes, I can cook **quite well**.*
   Can you dance? 5
S3: *No, I can't. Can you dance?*

very well/ fast	95%
quite well/ fast	70%
not very well/fast	40%
no	0%

HELLO!

● Can (making requests)

14 **Fill in the speech bubbles with sentences from the list.**

Can you help me up, please?
Can you give this to Mr Harris, please?
Can you read this for me, please?
Can you open your books at page 7, please?

15 🔲 **Read the dialogue and fill in the missing words. Then, listen and check. In pairs, act out similar dialogues using your name, address and phone number.**

A: Good morning, madam. Can I help you?
B: Yes please. I'd like to join the tennis club.
A: Certainly, madam. What's your 1) *name* ?
B: Mavis Steed.
A: Can you spell it, please?
B: Yes, of course. M - A - V - I - S ... S - T - double E - D.
A: And 2) *how old* are you?
B: I'm thirty-two years old.
A: Right. 3) *what's* your home address?
B: 7, Green Street.
A: Thanks. And your phone number?
B: 720644. *Thank you for coming*
A: 4) ...., Ms Steed. Here's your card. Please, sign it here.

● Spelling

16 🔲 **Listen to the dialogue and repeat it. Then, in pairs, use the prompts below to make similar dialogues, as in the example.**

A: What's your name, please?
B: *Anna Hughes*.
A: How do you spell it?
B: *A - double N - A . . . H - U - G - H - E - S*.

1 ...*Anna Hughes*...
2 ...Jimmy Stuart...
3 ...Wendy Clarke...
4 ...Vivienne Brown...
5 ...Frank Williams...
6 ...Quentin Phillips...

● Vocabulary revision

17 **Fill in the correct word(s).**

1 He hasn't got long hair. He's got ....*short*.... hair.
2 She hasn't got dark hair. She's got ....*brown*.... hair.
3 Sarah and Kate are twenty-four ....*years*.... old.
4 Gordon isn't ....*too tall*.... . He's short.
5 He hasn't got big eyes. He's got ....*small*.... eyes.
6 Tony is short and <u>slim</u> and he ....*has*.... a beard.
7 ....*and Hand*.... you dance well?
8 Hope to ....*hear*.... from you soon.
9 I ....*leave*.... in Edinburgh, Scotland.
10 He can run quite ....*very well*.... .

18 **Match the sentences to the pictures. Which express ability? Which express a polite request?**

a Can you tell me how much it is, please?
b Ann can use the computer very well.
c Billy can play the trumpet.
d Can you sign here, please?

• Vocabulary Revision Game

19 Work in two teams. Take it in turns to choose words from the list and make sentences. Each correct answer gets one point. The team with the most points is the winner.

slim, full lips, moustache, straight hair, beard, with, wavy, well-built, speak Italian, yellowish complexion, skin, flattish nose, swim, slanting eyes, quite fast, sign, very well, very dark skin

• Communication

20 a. Greetings

Listen to the dialogues and fill in the missing words. Listen again and repeat. In pairs, act out the dialogues.

- **A:** Good morning, Paul. **1)** ...*How*... are you?
  B: Very well, thanks. And **2)** ...*you*...?
  A: I'm fine.

- **A:** Hello. How are things?
  B: **3)** ...*Good*..., thanks. How are you?
  A: All right.

- **A:** Hi! How are you?
  B: **4)** ...*I'm not to*... bad. And you?
  A: Okay.

b. Saying Goodbye

Read and fill in the speech bubbles with the sentences below.

You too. Goodbye.   *Bye, Mum. See you.*

Now, listen and repeat. Finally, close your books and act out similar dialogues in pairs.

Bye. See you later.

Goodbye. Have a nice evening.

Pronunciation

21 Listen and tick. Listen again and repeat.

	/ iː /	/ ɪ /
six		
read		
three		

	/ iː /	/ ɪ /
slim		
teacher		
singer		

Writing

Complete the table with information about *yourself*, then write an Internet advertisement for a pen-friend. Use the texts in Ex. 4 as a model. Start with: *Hello!/Hi!*... Finish with: *Please e-mail me today./Please, be my e-mail pen pal/Hope to hear from you soon.*

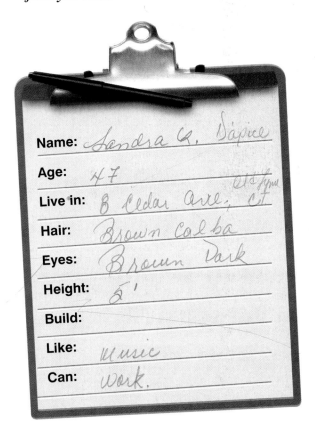

Name: Sandra Q. Dapice
Age: 47
Live in: 8 Cedar Ave, CT
Hair: Brown Colba
Eyes: Brown Dark
Height: 5'
Build:
Like: Music
Can: Work.

Words of Wisdom

Read these sentences. What do they mean?

- A friend in need is a friend indeed.
- Lend your money and lose your friend.

UNIT 3

Lead-in

1 a) **Look at the picture and fill in the gaps with the correct letters.**
b) **Where is each room?** *The study is in the attic.*

on the ground floor: the living-room *C* the dining-room *B*, the kitchen *A*.
on the first floor: the main bedroom *D*, the bathroom *E*, the child's bedroom *F*.
in the attic: the study *G*. **outside the house:** the garage *H*.

2 a) **Fill in the gaps with the correct numbers.** b) **What is there in each room?** *There is a sofa in the living-room.*
There are some chairs in the dining-room.

living-room: sofa *9*, fireplace *11*, table *10*, armchair *12*
dining-room: dining-table *6*, chairs *7*, mirror *8*
kitchen: fridge *2*, dishwasher *1*, cupboards *4*, sink *5*, cooker *3*
main bedroom: double bed *14*, wardrobe *13*
bathroom: bath *15*, washbasin *16*, toilet *17*
child's bedroom: single bed *19*, bedside cabinet *18*
study: desk *20*, bookcase *22*, chair *21*

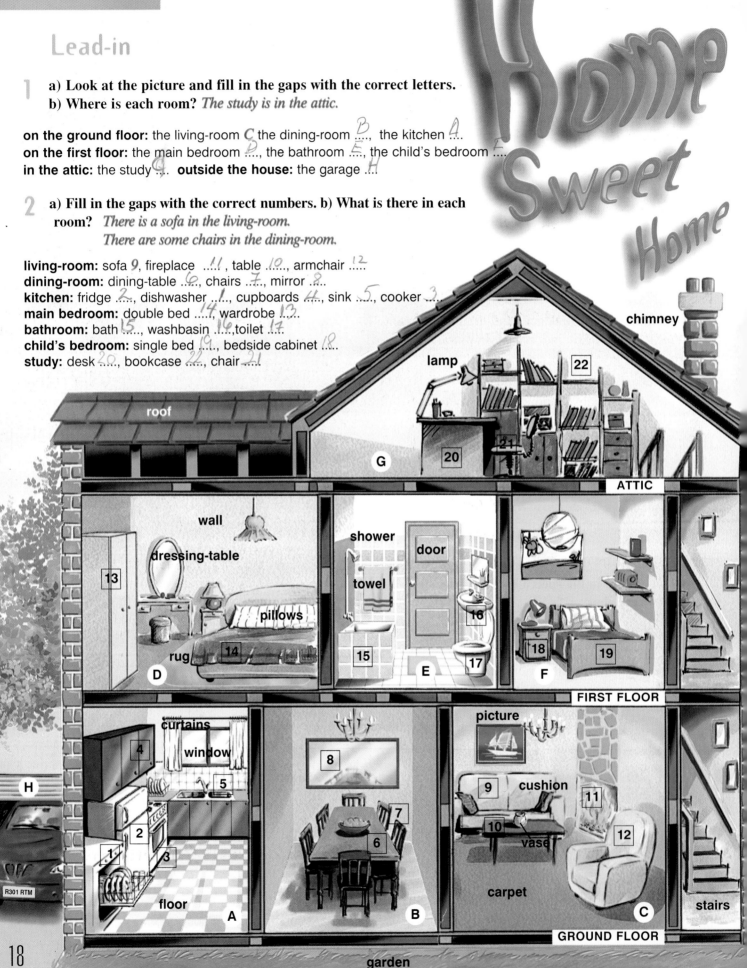

18

3 🔊 **First read the sentences and explain the meaning of the words in bold, then listen and underline the correct word.**

A. The house

a The house is quite ***expensive*/*cheap***.
b Upstairs there are ***three*/*four*** bedrooms.
c The house has also got a beautiful ***garage*/*garden***.

B. The flat

d The flat is rather ***big*/*small***.
e The flat has got a big ***balcony*/ *swimming-pool***.

Reading

4 **Read the texts and explain the words in bold. How many rooms are there in each place? What is there in each room? What else has each place got?**

Ⓐ *For Sale £370,000*

Address: 11, Hawk's Lane, Canterbury

This **lovely** house is half a mile from the city centre, and is near the shops and the main road. It is quite expensive, but it is very large. Upstairs, there are three bedrooms, each with a wardrobe and a bathroom. There is also a study with a big bookcase. Downstairs, there is a small bathroom with a shower and a toilet, a **huge** kitchen, a dining-room and a **spacious** living-room with a fireplace. The house has also got a **beautiful** garden and a swimming-pool.

Ⓑ *For Rent £180/month*

Address: 6, Shell Street, Canterbury

This **attractive** flat is in a **quiet** street near the city centre. It is rather small, but it is in a very **pleasant** area. It is also very cheap. It has got a **pretty** bedroom, a bathroom with a shower and a toilet, a **modern** kitchen with a cooker, a dishwasher and a fridge, and a **comfortable** living-room. The flat has also got a big balcony with a **wonderful** view. There is a **large** garage behind the building.

• Speaking

Read the texts again and make notes under the following headings, then look at the notes and talk about the two places.

Type of Home - Location - Cost - Size - Inside the House/Flat (Rooms, Furniture etc) - Outside the House/Flat

Language Development

• Vocabulary

5 **Look at the adjectives in bold in the texts in Ex. 4 and fill in the nouns which are used with them.**

lovely *house*	attractive *flat*	modern *kitchen*
huge *kitchen*	quiet *street*	comfortable *livis*
spacious *livingroom*	pleasant *area*	wonderful *view*
beautiful *garden*	pretty *bedroom*	large *garage* *behind the b*

6 **Fill in the adjectives which have a similar meaning. Choose adjectives from the list above.**

big = huge, *spacious, large*
beautiful = attractive, *pretty*
pleasant = *living, wonderful*

• Grammar: Plurals

There is - There are

7   **Study the following, then complete the rules.**

Singular		Plural	Singular		Plural
chair	→	chair**s**	addre**ss**	→	address**es**
room	→	room**s**	bu**s**	→	bus**es**
wall	→	wall**s**	bru**sh**	→	brush**es**
table	→	table**s**	ben**ch**	→	bench**es**

Most nouns take *-s* in the plural.
Nouns ending in .... take *-es* in the plural.

SINGULAR	PLURAL
[NEAR] ☞ **This** is a chair. [FAR] ☞ **That** is a clock.	[NEAR] ☞ **These** are chairs. [FAR] ☞ **Those** are clocks.

• We use ***this/these*** for things near us. We use ..../........................... for things far from us.
these

8   **Write sentences, as in the example.**

1 ☞  and ☞

This is a sofa and that is a table.

2 ☞ and ☞

~~This is Desk~~ ~~These are chairs~~

3 ☞ and ☞

~~This is bench~~ ~~These are Lamps~~

4 ☞ and ☞

~~This is T.V~~ ~~These are an Pillows~~

5 ☞ and ☞

~~This is Bookcase~~ ~~That is a fire place~~

6 ☞ and ☞

~~This is Stove~~ ~~That is a Dishwasher~~

---

9   **Study the table, then complete the rules.**

Singular		Plural
there **is** *a/an* ...	**AFFIRMATIVE**	there **are** *some* ...
there **isn't** *a/an* ...	**NEGATIVE**	there **aren't** *any* ...
Is there *a/an* ...?	**INTERROGATIVE**	**Are** there *any* ...?
Yes, there **is**. **No**, there **isn't**.	**SHORT ANSWERS**	**Yes**, there **are**. **No**, there **aren't**.

We use **there** ....*is*........ in the singular.
***There is** a **bed** in the bedroom.*
We use **there** ....*are*........ in the plural.
***There are** two **beds** in the bedroom.*
We use **some** in the plural in the affirmative.
***There are** some chairs in the kitchen.*
We use *no future out* in the plural in the negative and interrogative.
***There aren't** **any** chairs in the kitchen.*
***Are there** **any** chairs in the kitchen?*

10   **What things can you see in the picture below? Put a tick (✓) or a cross (✗) for each, then talk about the room, as in the examples.**

dining-table ..✓.., armchair ..✗.., pictures ..✓.., posters ..✗..,
rug ✓.., sofa ✗.., chairs ✓.., cupboards ✗.., vase .....,
mirror ..✗.., curtains ..✓.., beds ..✗.., flowers ....., pillows ✗..

*There is a dining-table **but there isn't** an armchair.*
*There are some pictures **but there aren't** any posters.*

• Prepositions of Place

ON   IN   UNDER   BEHIND   NEXT TO   IN FRONT OF

1 First, look at the picture, then read the short text and underline the correct prepositions.

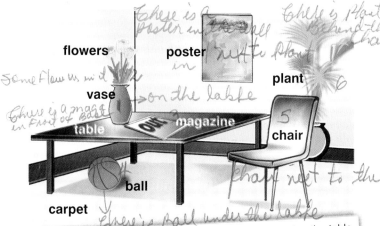

flowers   poster   plant

vase   table   magazine   chair

ball

carpet

There is a table in the room. There is a vase **(1) in/on** the table with some flowers **(2) in/on** it. There is a magazine **(3) under/in front of** the vase. There is a ball **(4) behind/under** the table. There is a chair **(5) next to/under** the table. There is a plant **(6) behind/in front of** the chair. There is a poster **(7) on/in** the wall **(8) next to/under** the plant.

[handwritten notes overlaid on picture: "There is a poster in the wall", "There is Plant Behind the chair", "in next to Plant", "Some Flowers in a vase", "on the table", "There is a magazine in front of vase", "Chair next to the table", "There is Ball under the table"]

2 *This is Sally's living-room.* Ask and answer questions using the prompts below.

1	pictures/wall?	6	table/sofa?
2	armchair/fireplace?	7	magazines/table?
3	plants/sofa?	8	cushions/sofa?
4	fireplace/mirror?	9	posters/wall?
5	fridge/living-room?	10	vases/table?

SA: Are there any pictures on the wall?
SB: Yes, there are. There are some pictures on the wall.

[handwritten at bottom: "SA. are there any armchair next to the fire place SB. yes there are. There are one Sofa nextto fire place SA. are there a sofa. behind"]

3 Look at the picture and read the text, then fill in *next to, on, behind* or *under*. Finally, ask and answer questions, as in the example.

S1: Where is the carpet?
S2: It's on the floor. Where is the pillow?

This is Jenny's bedroom. It's nice and spacious with a carpet **1)** .... the floor. There is a very comfortable bed with a pillow **2)** .... it. **3)** .... the bed there are two windows. There is a lamp **4)** .... the bed. Jenny's desk is quite modern. There is a chair **5)** .... it and some magazines **6)** .... it. Jenny has got some pictures and a poster **7)** .... the walls. There is also a bedside table. **8)** .... the poster. Jenny likes her bedroom a lot.

[handwritten fill-ins: 1) On, 2) On the Bed, 3) Comfortable, 4) at, 6) on the floor, 7) on, 8) Next to the poster]

Writing (Project)

Look at the Photo File section and complete Paula's letter to her friend telling her about her new flat and her favourite room.

Pronunciation

4 🔊 Listen and tick. Listen again and repeat.

	/ ɑː /	/ æ /
attic		
garden		
carpet		

	/ ɑː /	/ æ /
plant		
armchair		
flat		

3 Home Sweet Home

1

• Reading & Listening

15 **a) Look at the pictures. Which shows:** *a mud hut?/a chalet?/a block of flats?/a farmhouse?/a houseboat?*

b) Listen and match the people's names to their homes. Write *S* for Salif, *M* for Maria, *G* for Greg, *P* for Paul and *H* for Hendrick.

c) Read the texts and fill in the missing prepositions.

2

3

4

5

1 Salif lives .... a village .... Nigeria. He lives .... a mud hut. Mud huts have got grass roofs. They have usually got only one room.

2 Maria lives in a chalet .... a mountain .... Switzerland. These houses are made of wood. They have usually got two floors and an attic.

3 Greg lives .... a huge block of flats .... Boston. His flat is .... the fifteenth floor and it is in the centre of the city. He lives .... 332, Newbury Street. There are a lot of expensive shops .... the area.

4 Paul lives .... a farm .... Canada. He lives .... a big farmhouse near a river.

5 Hendrick lives .... a houseboat .... a river in Holland. It's got three cabins.

16 *Sandra Richway is talking to an estate agent.* **Read the dialogue and try to fill in the missing information.**

Listen to the cassette and check your answers. Finally, in pairs, read the dialogue aloud.

A: Hello. **1)** ....?
S: Yes. I want to rent a flat in this area.
A: Okay, let me see. There is a very nice flat for rent quite near the city centre.
S: **2)** *How many* .... rooms has it got?
A: It has got a living-room, dining-room, kitchen, bathroom and two bedrooms. So that's six rooms.
S: And how much is it?
A: It's quite a good price — £300 per month.
S: That sounds perfect. **3)** ....?
A: It's 14, Oakfield View.
S: **4)** .... ?
A: Yes, it's O - A - K - F - I - E - L - D ... V - I - E - W.
S: **5)** .... see it ?
A: Of course. I can take you there right now. Have you got time?
S: Yes. That's great.
A: Okay. I've got the keys here, so let's go.

• Communication: Addresses and Phone Numbers

17 **Listen and repeat. Then, in pairs, act out similar dialogues using the prompts below.**

A: What's your address, please?
B: *14, Milcote Road, Birmingham.*
A: Can you spell the street name, please?
B: *M - I - L - C - O - T - E.*
A: Thank you. Have you got a telephone number?
B: Yes. It's *4204188.*

- *12, Longhurst Lane, Reading (Tel.: 535602)*
- *17, Morrison Avenue, Bath (Tel.: 334598)*
- *21, Primrose Street, Crewe (Tel.: 750559)*

18 🔲 **a)** *Karen and Tom want to rent a house or flat. Look at the pictures, then listen to the cassette and say which place they want.*

🔲 **b)** **Read the advertisements, then listen again and underline the correct word in bold. Now, using the advertisements, describe the two places. Start like this:** *This lovely house is five miles from the city centre. It is very expensive, but it is very large. Upstairs, there are ...*

For Rent £800/month

6, Sandon Street

Lovely house five miles from city centre

* Upstairs -
  4 bedrooms; 2 bathrooms (bath, shower, toilet)
* Downstairs -
  1) *spacious/small* living-room; kitchen; dining-room; study; small **2)** *bedroom/ bathroom*

* large **3)** *garden/swimming-pool*; double garage

For Rent £300/month

8, Chamberlain Street

Attractive **4)** *flat/chalet* near city centre

* 2 bedrooms; 1 large bathroom (bath, shower, toilet); modern kitchen; comfortable living-room; **5)** *dining-room/study*

* small garden; **6)** *garage/swimming-pool*

• Vocabulary Revision Game

19 **Work in two teams. Take it in turns to choose words from the list and make sentences. Each correct sentence gets one point. The team with the most points is the winner.**

ground floor, attic, wardrobe, huge, quiet, behind, view, under, comfortable, expensive, cooker, some, carpet, study, swimming-pool, balcony, there aren't any

• Memory Game

20 **Work in two teams. Look at the picture of the house on p. 18 for one minute, then close your books and say what there is in each room. Each correct answer gets one point. The team with the most points is the winner.**

Writing (advertisements for houses)

Use the information in Ex. 18 to write two short advertisements (50 - 80 words each) similar to those in Ex. 4. Use the pictures from the Photo File section and the plan below.

Plan

For Rent: ....
Address: ....

- type of place
- where
- cost
- size
- inside the house/flat (rooms, furniture, etc)
- outside the house/flat

Words of Wisdom

Read these sentences. What do they mean?

* Home is where the heart is.
* There is no place like home.
* East, west, home is best.

The Loch Ness Monster

Sandra Manning and David Parr are reporters. They work for *The Morning Sun* in London. Mike Battle is the editor of the newspaper.

IN "THE MORNING SUN" OFFICES...

Sandra! David! Look at this.

What is it, Mike?

There are stories about the Loch Ness Monster in all the papers today, but there aren't any photographs! Go to Loch Ness. I want a story and photographs with it!

ON THE TRAIN...

Is there really a monster, David?

Maybe!

AT LOCH NESS...

Can you see the monster?

No, I can't. Let's hire a boat and look for it.

VROOOOM

AFTER THREE HOURS ON THE BOAT...

Sandra! Look! The monster! Can you see it? Wow! It's huge!

Where is it? I can't see it! Quick, take some photographs!

Sandra, be careful! Sit down! Don't stand up!

OH NO! HELP!!!! DAVID!!! HELP ME!

1 **Look at the pictures on p. 24 and point to** *the editor, the reporters* **and** *the monster.* **What do you know about the Loch Ness monster?**

2 🔈 **Listen and put the sentences in the order you hear them.**

Let's hire a boat and look for it. ....
Sandra, be careful! ....
Go to Loch Ness. ....

3 **Read the episode, then mark the sentences as T (true) or F (false).**

1 David is the editor. ......
2 There are photographs of the monster in all the papers. ......
3 The monster is huge. ......
4 Sandra can see the monster. ......

4 **Fill in** *on* **or** *in.*

1 David and Sandra are ...... the office.
2 Mike's got newspapers ...... his hand.
3 There are stories about the monster ...... all the papers.
4 Sandra and David are ...... the train.
5 Sandra and David are ...... a boat.

The Imperative

We use **the imperative** to give orders or instructions. We form affirmative orders or instructions with the **base form of the verb.** *Look at this.*
We form negative orders or instructions with **don't + base form of the verb.** *Don't stand up.*

5 **Read the episode again and find eight sentences which are orders. Who says each sentence?**
Look at this. (Mike)

Personal Pronouns

Subject pronouns (*I, you, he, she, it, we, you, they*) go before verbs as their subjects. **Object pronouns** (*me, you, him, her, it, us, you, them*) go after verbs as their objects.
Look at **her.** *She's Sandra.*

6 **Look at the pictures and make sentences using object pronouns, as in the example.** *Look at her!*

7 **Fill in the speech bubbles with sentences from the list.**
● *Don't be afraid!* ● *Don't worry. It's gone.* ● *Take my hand!*
● *Put this on.*

8 **Complete the puzzle to find Mike's job.**

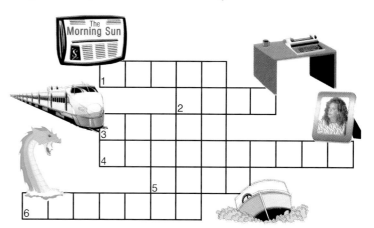

9 🔈 **Listen to the episode, then take roles and read it aloud.**

10 **Read the paragraph and fill in the missing words.**

Mike Battle is the **1) e** *d i t o r* of *The Morning Sun*. David and Sandra are reporters. In the office, Mike shows David and Sandra some **2) p** _ _ _ _ _ . There are stories about Nessie, the **3) m** _ _ _ _ _ _ in Loch Ness, in all of them. David and Sandra go to Scotland on a **4) t** _ _ _ _ . They want to take **5) p** _ _ _ _ _ _ _ _ _ of Nessie. There are **6) b** _ _ _ _ by the loch. David and Sandra hire one to **7) l** _ _ _ for Nessie. After three **8) h** _ _ _ _ on the boat, David sees the monster behind Sandra.

Writing

Write descriptions of Mike, Sandra and David.

25

UNIT 4

Like Father, like Son

1 ....
2 ....
6 ....
3 ....
4 ....
5 ....
Tony

Lead-in

1 **Look at the picture. Who's Tony's father? mother? grandfather? grandmother? sister? brother?**

2 **Describe the people in the picture.**

3 🔊 **First read the sentences, then listen and underline the correct word.**

a I live in **Montreal/Madrid**.
b There are **seventy/seven** of us in our family.
c My father is a **surgeon/teacher**.
d He works at the local **hospital/school**.
e I don't like going to the **cinema/theatre**.

Reading

4 *Pièrre has got a letter. It's from his new pen-friend, Tony.*

Read Tony's letter and a) fill in the names of the people in the picture; b) answer the questions below; c) explain the words in bold.

1 What does Tony look like?
2 What is his mother's job?
3 Where is Tony's house?
4 What does Tony like/not like doing? *Deng To the Cinema Theatre*
5 How does the letter start/finish?

43, St Catherine Street
Montreal, PQ
M3B 2Y7
Canada

Dear Pierre,
  I'm Tony Philips and I'm seventeen years old. I'm a student and I **live** in Montreal, Canada. I'm tall and slim with short dark hair and brown eyes.
  There are seven of us in our family; my **grandparents**, Steve and Sally, my **parents**, Joe and Kate, my sister, Liz, **aged** nine, my brother, Leo, aged six, and **of course**, me. My father is a **surgeon**. He works at the **local hospital** and my mother is a teacher in a **primary school**. We live in a big house about twenty minutes from the **city centre**.
  In my **free time**, I love playing computer games and listening to rock music. I'm an **MTV maniac**. My favourite group is Guns'n'Roses. Do you like them? I also like going to the cinema. I go to the cinema every Saturday. I don't like going to the theatre, though.
  Well, that's all about me. **Write back** and tell me about **yourself**.

Best wishes,
Tony

26

• Speaking

Read the letter again and complete the table. Then, look at your notes and talk about Tony. Start like this:

Tony Philips is seventeen years old. ...

FULL NAME:	*Tony Philips*
AGE/OCCUPATION:	*17 years old, student Occup.*
CITY/COUNTRY:	*Montreal, Canada*
APPEARANCE:	*Tall, Slim, Short Dark Hair*
FAMILY MEMBERS:	*grandparents: Steve and Sally* *parents: Joe (surgeon) and Kate (teacher)* *sister: Liz (nine)* *brother: Leo (six)*
HOME:	*43 St Catherine Street* *Montreal, PQ, M3B 2Y7* *Canada*
LIKES/LOVES:	*playing computer games,*

Language Development

• Vocabulary

5 **Fill in** *niece, grandmother, wife, sister, daughter* **or** *aunt*, **as in the example.**

1 husband - ...*wife*...
2 son - *daughter*
3 uncle - *Aunt*

4 nephew - *niece*
5 brother - *sister*
6 grandfather - *grandmother*

6 📼 **Fill in the missing days of the week, then listen and repeat.**

Sunday, Friday, Tuesday

1 Monday, 2 *Tuesday*, 3 Wednesday, 4 Thursday,
5 *Friday*, 6 Saturday, 7 *Sunday*

7 **a) Match the free-time activities to the pictures. Not all the activities match the pictures.**

a) listening to (rock/classical/pop/jazz) music, b) walking in the park, c) going on a picnic, d) going to the cinema, e) travelling, f) exercising, g) reading, h) fishing, i) playing football, j) camping, k) playing the guitar, l) watching TV

b) Use the list of activities above and the verbs below to make sentences, as in the example.

love (♥ ♥)　　like (♥)　　don't like (✗)　　hate (✗ ✗)

*I like fishing and I love reading. I don't like camping **though**.*
OR
*I like fishing and I love reading, **but** I don't like camping.*

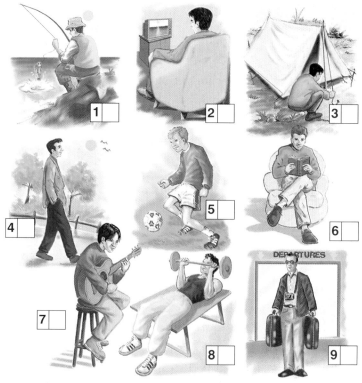

1 ☐　2 ☐　3 ☐
4 ☐　5 ☐　6 ☐
7 ☐　8 ☐　9 ☐

• Grammar: Possessive Case

8 **Read the examples and study the rules, then underline the correct items in the sentences below.**

the boy's ball

the girls' ball

Ann and John's mother

- We add **'s** when a noun is singular to show possession. *This is the boy's ball.* We add **'** when a noun is plural and ends in -s to show possession. *This is the girls' ball.*
- We add **'s** to the last noun of a phrase to show possession. *This is Ann and John's mother.*

1 This is my **son's/sons** bicycle.
2 This is **Jenny/Jenny's** desk.
3 That is **Tony and Pam's/Tony's and Pam** house.
4 Those are **Bob/Bob's** shoes.
5 These are the **boys/boys'** bicycles.

• Grammar:

Personal Pronouns & Possessive Adjectives

9 Fill in *her, me, him, my* or *their*.

Subject Pronouns	I	you	he	she	it	we	you	they
Object Pronouns	....	you	....	her	it	us	you	them
Possessive Adjectives	....	your	his	....	its	our	your	....

10 Read the text and underline the examples of the possessive case and the possessive adjectives.

Bill & Carol

John   Ann   Helen   Peter

Lisa   Dave

Hi! I'm Lisa and I'm seven. John and Ann are my parents. Helen is my father's sister. She is my aunt. Peter is her husband. He's my uncle. Their son's name is Dave. He's five years old. He's my cousin. Bill and Carol are our grandparents. They are John and Helen's parents.

11 Look at the family tree in Ex. 10 and complete the sentences.

1 Dave is *John and Ann's* nephew. He is *their* nephew.
2 Lisa is ......*Dave*...... cousin. She is ...*his*... cousin.
3 Lisa is ......*Helen*...................... niece.
   She is ......*Helen*............ niece.
4 Helen is ...*Peter's*.... wife. She is ...*his*.... wife.
5 Peter is ...*Lisa*.... uncle. He is ...*her*.... uncle.
6 Ann is ......*Dave*...... aunt. She is ...*his*.... aunt.
7 Bill is ...*Carol*.... husband. He is ...*her*... husband.

28

Who's ...? = Who is ...? ***Who's*** Lisa?
Whose ...? is used to ask who the possessor is.
Whose is this ball?

12 Fill in *who's, whose, him, them, her* or *me*.

1 "...*Whose*... dog is it?" "Lyn's."
2 "...*who is*... Lisa?" "She's Dave's cousin."
3 "...*whose*...niece is Pam?" "Ann and Bob's."
4 "...*Who's*... Sally's brother?" "John."
5 "Help ...*me*...! I can't open the door."
6 "Ask ...*him*... . He can help you."
7 "...*Whose*... house is it?" "It's Steven's."
8 "Look at ...*them*... . They're very tall."
9 "Give this to ...*her*... . It's hers."
10 "...*who's*... James?" "He's my uncle."

• Speaking

a) Look at Lisa's family tree. Ask and answer questions with *who's* or *whose*.

S1: *Who's Dave?*
S2: *He's Lisa's cousin. Whose son is John?*
S3: *He's Carol and Bill's son.*

b) Point to students and objects in your classroom and make sentences using object pronouns.

S1: *Look at* **them**. *They're desks.*
S2: *Look at* **her**. *She's Mary.*

• Guessing Game

13 Write on the board some of your relatives' names (e.g. *Tony, Paula, Tom, Philip, Kathy*). **The class in two teams, try to guess who each person is, as in the example. The teams win one point for each correct guess. The team with the most points is the winner.**

Team A S1: *Is Tony your father?*
You: *No, he isn't.*

Team B S1: *Is he your uncle?*
You: *Yes, he is. etc.*

• Writing **(Project)**

Draw your family tree and write a short text like the one in Ex. 10. Decorate your project with pictures of your family.

Grammar: Possessive Pronouns

14 Fill in *ours, yours,* or *hers*.

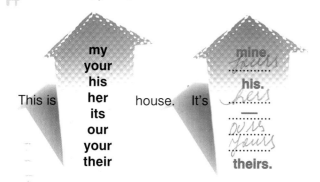

This is **my your his her its our your their** house. It's *mine.* *hers.* *ours.* *yours.* **theirs.**

! Possessive adjectives come before a noun.
*It's **my** dog.*
Possessive pronouns don't take a noun after them.
*It's **mine**. (NOT: It's mine book.)*

15 Match the people to the objects. Then, in pairs, ask and answer questions, as in the example.

PEOPLE

Peter
Lyn
Sam
Tom

OBJECTS

passport
bicycle
ball
bag

SA: ***Whose** bag is this?*
SB: *I think it's **Lyn's**. Yes, it's **hers**.*

16 Underline the correct word(s).

1 "***Who's**/Whose is Ann?*" "*She's **my**/mine sister.*"
2 "*Is this bag **your**/yours?*" "*No, it's **Sheila's**/Sheila.*"
3 "***Who/Whose** dog is this?*" "*It's **their**/theirs.*"
4 "*Are those balls **your**/yours?*" "*Yes, they're **our**/ours.*"
5 "*Who's he?*" "***Tom's and Julie's**/Tom and Julie's father.*"

Grammar: Present Simple

17 Study the table, then complete the rules.

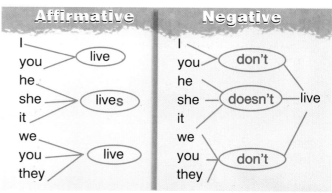

Affirmative	Negative
I you he she it we you they	I you he she it we you they
live / lives / live	don't / doesn't / don't — live

- Most verbs take ...**s**... in the affirmative third person singular. *I live - he lives*
- We use *doesn't* + **the base form of the verb** to form the **negative third person singular**. In all other persons we use ...*don't*... *he **doesn't** live - I **don't** live*

Spelling

- Most verbs ending in **-ss, -sh, -ch, -x** and **-o** take **-es** in the third person singular. *I finish ≥ he finishes*
- Verbs ending in a **consonant + y** drop the -y and take **-ies** in the third person singular. *I study ≥ he studies* (BUT: *I play — he plays*)

18 Fill in the correct form of the verb.

1 I go - he ......*goes*......   4 I wash - he ...*washes*...
2 I work - he ...*works*...   5 I fly - he ...*flies*...
3 I love - he ...*loves*...   6 I enjoy - he ...*enjoys*...

Use

We use the **present simple** for permanent states, repeated actions and daily routines.
*He **lives** in Madrid. (permanent state)*
*She **goes** to the cinema on Saturdays.*
(repeated action - routine)

19 Underline the present simple verb forms in the text in Ex. 4.

20 **Study the table. How do we form questions and short answers?**

Interrogative			Short answers
Do	I you	live ...?	Yes, I/you do. No, I/you don't.
Does	he she it	live ...?	Yes, he/she/it does. No, he/she/it doesn't.
Do	we you they	live ...?	Yes, we/you/they do. No, we/you/they don't.

21 **Fill in *do*, *does*, *don't* or *doesn't*.**

1 A: *Do* .... you live in Madrid?
B: No, I *don't* .
2 A: *Does* .... Tim like watching TV?
B: Yes, he *does* .
3 A: *Do* .... they live in a flat?
B: Yes, they *Do* .
4 A: *Does* .... Mary work in a hospital?
B: No, she *Doesn't* .
5 A: *Does* .... she like playing tennis?
B: Yes, she *Does* .
6 A: *Do* .... they go fishing on Sundays?
B: No, they *Don't* .
7 A: *Does* .... he work in a school?
B: No, he *Doesn't* .
8 A: *Do* .... you get up late on Sundays?
B: Yes, we *Do* .
9 A: *Do* .... they like playing football?
B: Yes, they *Do* .
10 A: *Does* .... she like listening to jazz music?
B: No, she *Doesn't* .

Pronunciation

22 📼 **Listen and tick. Listen again and repeat.**

	/ s /	/ z /	/ ɪz /
lives			
walks			
goes			
writes			
washes			
watches			

23 a) **Look at the table below and the key. Which day(s) does Helen *love/like/not like/hate*?** *Helen hates Mondays.*
b) 📼 **Now, listen and tick (✓) the days Helen does the following activities. Then, ask and answer questions, as in the example.**

S1: *Why does Helen hate Mondays?*
S2: *Helen hates Mondays because she gets up very early. Why does she like Tuesdays?...*

Helen	Mon	Tue	Wed	Thu	Fri	Sat	Sun
	✗ ✗	♥	✗	✗	♥	♥	♥♥
get up very early	hate	like	not like	not like	Like	Like	Love
get up very late	hate	Like	no Like	no Like	Like	Like	Love
go to the cinema					Like	Like	Love
meet friends							
go shopping							
do the ironing							
clean the house							

24 **Read the letter and explain the adjectives in bold. Which adjectives describe appearance? Which describe character?**

Dear Sarah,

My name is Nora Smith. I am sixteen years old and I live in Swansea, in Wales.

There are five of us in our family. My father, Brett, is an artist. He's a very **kind** person. My mother, Emily, is an actress. She's very **beautiful** with fair hair and **gorgeous** green eyes. She's also very **patient**. My brother, Mark, is fifteen. He's got brown hair and blue eyes. He is **good-looking**, but he's a bit **lazy** and **rude**. My sister, Melanie, is twelve with fair hair and **lovely** green eyes. She's **pretty** and **clever** but she's a bit **bossy**.
Please write soon and tell me about your family.

Best wishes,
Nora

Now talk about your family.

1 What do your father, mother, brother and sister look like?

2 Can you describe their characters?

My father Looks like very kind Black Hair Browing eyes! my mother Died six years ago,

My Brother and Sister, are Bery Beautiful

They are very nice and calm people

25 📼 **Study the descriptions, then listen and fill in the missing words. In pairs, ask and answer questions, as in the example.**

SA: *What does Philip look like?*
SB: *He's good-looking with short fair hair and green eyes. What is he like?*
SA: *He's lazy.*

Name: Philip
Appearance:
1) *Good Looking* short fair hair, green eyes
Character:
2) *Lazy*

Name: Miss Adams
Appearance:
3) *She's Good Looking* long blonde hair, blue eyes
Character:
4) *crazy*

Name: Jean
Appearance:
5) *Nice Looking* short brown hair, brown eyes.
Character:
6) *Funny*
I Just Looking

• Vocabulary Revision Game

26 **Work in two teams. Take it in turns to choose words from the list and make sentences. Each correct sentence gets one point. The team with the most points is the winner.**

family, live, lazy, city centre, clever, parents, camping, husband, rude, aunt, uncle, cousin, niece, bossy, lovely, good-looking, patient, kind, gorgeous

• Communication: Identifying People

27 📼 **Read the dialogue, then listen and fill in the missing adjectives. Which girl in the picture is Steve's sister? Listen again and follow the dialogue. Then, in pairs, act it out.**

B: Wow! Look at that girl, Steve!
S: Which girl?
B: That girl. She's really 1) *Pretty*.
S: Which girl? Where?
B: The one over there, with the 2) *Blonde* hair.
S: I can't see her.
B: Yes you can! She's on the bench.
S: Do you mean the girl in the dark T-shirt?
B: No! Not her — the one next to her.
S: Oh, I can see her now.
B: Isn't she 3) *Pretty*?
S: Mmm, not bad. She's very 4) *Pretty*, too.
B: Do you know her?
S: Yes, I do actually. She's my sister.

Writing (a letter to a pen-friend)

Use the letter in Ex. 4 as a model and the plan below to write a letter to your pen-friend.

Plan

Dear + (your pen-friend's first name),

Introduction
Para 1: Say who you are, how old you are, what your occupation is, where you live and what you look like.

Main Body
Para 2: Talk about your family (members, ages, jobs) and your house.
Para 3: Say what you like/don't like doing.

Conclusion
Para 4: Ask your pen-friend to write back soon.

Best wishes,
(your first name)

Words of Wisdom

Read these sentences. What do they mean?

- Like father, like son/Like mother, like daughter.
- The apple never falls far from the tree.

• Vocabulary

1 Fill in the correct country or nationality.

1 Argentina .... *Buenos aires* ....
2 .... Brazilian
3 Spain .... *Portugal* ....
4 Mexico .... *Mexico city* ....
5 .... Greek
6 .... Finnish
7 Turkey ....
8 *Montreal* .... Canadian
9 Japan .... *Tokio* ....
10 .... Scottish

(10 marks)

2 Fill in the correct word.

hear, near, going, College, dancer, spacious, cheap, e-mail, yellowish, view

1 Downstairs, there is a ...... *spacious* ...... living-room.
2 Tony loves ...... *going* ...... to the cinema.
3 Please be my ...... *e-mail* ...... pen pal.
4 Hope to ...... *hear* ...... from you soon.
5 Rashid is a student at Mortimer ...... *College* ....
6 Bob's house is ...... *near* ...... the city centre.
7 We have got a wonderful ...... *view* ...... from our balcony.
8 This modern flat is a bargain. It's really very ...... *cheap* ......
9 Mary is quite tall and slim. She is a ...... *dancer* ....
10 Chinese people have usually got a ...... *yellowish* ...... complexion.

(10 marks)

3 Choose the correct item.

1 Beth isn't a very good student. She's very ...... *lazy* ....
   A rude **B** lazy **C** clever
2 Mr Cline works at the hospital. He is a(n) ...... *surgeon* ......
   A engineer **B** musician **C** surgeon
3 Is Jane's hair grey? No, it's ...... *fair* ....
   A fair **B** wavy **C** yellow
4 There are two ...... *mirrors* ...... in the bathroom.
   A sofas **B** mirrors **C** cookers
5 "...... *Whose* ...... magazine is that?" "It's Karen's."
   A Who's **B** Who **C** Whose
6 My sister goes to primary school. She's very ...... *young* ......
   A young **B** middle-aged **C** old

7 Kim is my sister's daughter. She's my ...... *niece* ......
   A nephew **B** niece **C** cousin
8 People from Sweden have got ...... *slanting eyes* ......
   A slanting eyes **B** dark brown skin
   C a pale complexion
9 There is a big ...... *sink* ...... in the kitchen.
   A bookcase **B** sink **C** washbasin
10 I like my teacher. She's always very ...... *patient* ....
   A bossy **B** rude **C** patient

(10 marks)

4 Fill in the missing preposition.

1 Prague is the capital ...... *of* ...... the Czech Republic.
2 He is well-built ...... *with* ...... short fair hair.
3 My pen pal is ...... *from* ...... Canada.
4 John lives ...... *in* ...... a huge block of flats.
5 There is a lovely poster ...... *on* ...... the wall.
6 Is there a fireplace ...... *in* ...... the living-room?
7 My father works ...... *at* ...... the local hospital.
8 The garden is ...... *at* ...... the house.

(8 marks)

• Grammar

5 Fill in the correct form of the verbs in brackets.

1 A: Where ...... *Does Juan* ...... (be) Juan from?
   B: He ...... *is* ...... (be) from Spain.
2 A: ...... *Do you* ...... (you/like) swimming?
   B: No, I ...... *Do not or I don't* ...... (do/not).
3 Jenny ...... *Does Jenny got* ...... (have/not) got curly hair.
   She ...... *Doesn't have* ...... (have) got straight hair.
4 Helen usually ...... *Does* ...... (watch) TV in the afternoons but Mark ...... *Does* ...... (listen) to music.
5 My English teacher ...... *is* ...... (be) very patient, but my Maths teacher ...... *is not* ...... (be/not).
6 A: ...... *Does he* ...... (Philip/live) in Madrid?
   B: Yes, he ...... *Does* ...... (do).
7 My father ...... (not/get up) early on Saturdays.
8 A: ...... (be) it a big house?
   B: Yes, there ...... (be) eight rooms in it.

(8 marks)

6 **Choose the correct word to fill in each gap.**

hers, my, she, him, his, her

1 A: Does she like tennis?
  B: Yes, it's ...*hers*... favourite sport.
2 A: Have you got a telephone number?
  B: Yes, ...*my*... number is 4241889.
3 A: Does he like football?
  B: Yes, it's ...*his*... favourite sport.
4 A: Is Beth your sister?
  B: No, ...*she*... is my cousin.
5 A: Is this Doug's book?
  B: Yes, give it to ...*him*... .
6 A: Is this Lisa's pencil?
  B: Yes, it's ...*hers*... .

(6 marks)

7 **Underline the correct word.**

1 My **son's**/**sons'** car is red.
2 Tina is **Lucy's and Bill's**/**Lucy and Bill's** aunt.
3 These are the **girls**/**girl's** bags.
4 Their **daughters'**/**daughter's** name is Kate.
5 Our **fathers'**/**father's** study is in the attic.

(5 marks)

● Communication

8 **Match the questions to the answers, as in the example.**

1 How old are you?	a Peter Jones.
2 Are you from London?	b Yes, of course. P-E-T-E-R ... J-O-N-E-S
3 What's your job?	c I'm 28 years old. *1*
4 What's your name?	d 21, Green Street.
5 Can you spell it, please?	e 8695980.
6 What's your home address?	f No, I'm not. I'm from Manchester.
7 What's your phone number?	g I'm a waiter. *3*

1 ..*c*.. 2 ..*f*.. 3 ..*g*.. 4 ..*a*.. 5 ..*b*.. 6 ..*d*.. 7 ..*e*..

(7 marks)

● Reading

9 **Read the letter and answer the questions below.**

Dear Jane,

  My name is Tony Wilson. I am thirteen years old and I live in Liverpool in England.
  There are five of us in our family. My father, John, is an artist. He's a very clever person and he's very kind. My mother, Elaine, is very beautiful. She is tall and slim with long straight fair hair and blue eyes. She's a very patient woman. My brother, Martin, is sixteen years old. He is tall with brown hair and blue eyes. He's quite lazy. My sister, Karen, is fifteen years old. She's short with green eyes. She is a bit bossy.
  Well, that's all about me. Please write soon and tell me about your family.

  Best wishes,
  Tony

1 How old is Tony? *13*
2 Where does he live? *Liverpool*
3 What is his father's job? *artist*
4 Can you describe his father's character? *clever*
5 What does his mother look like? *tall & slim*
6 Can you describe her character?
7 What does Martin look like? *Tall Brown Hair and Blue eyes*
8 Can you describe Martin's character? *Quite Lazy*
9 What does Karen look like? *Short, Green eyes*
10 Can you describe Karen's character? *Bit Bossy*

(10 marks)

Writing

10 **Circle the odd word.**

1 tall, short, (old,) well-built — man
2 young, dark, middle-aged, old — woman
3 brown, grey, pale, wavy — hair
4 wavy, curly, slanting, straight — hair
5 slanting, blue, brown, slim — eyes
6 pale, dark, wide, light — complexion
7 patient, beautiful, pretty, gorgeous — girl
8 lazy, kind, bossy, rude, curly — woman

(8 marks)

11 **Describe a member of your family. Talk about his/her physical appearance and character. Use words from Exs. 9 and 10.**

(18 marks)

TOTAL: *100 marks*

Day after Day

An Early Bird or a Night Owl?

Unit 5

- daily routines
- free-time activities

Birds of a Feather!

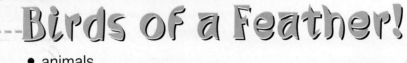

- animals

Unit 6

Module 2

Come Rain or Shine

Unit 7

◄ **Learn how to ...**
- tell the time
- ask about pets
- buy clothes
- order food
- accept/refuse offers

◄ **Practise ...**
- adverbs of frequency
- prepositions of time
- question words
- present continuous
- plurals
- countable/uncountable nouns
- how much/how many
- (a) few/(a) little
- a/an/some/any

- weather conditions
- clothes

Enjoy your Meal!

- types of food & drink
- kitchen equipment

Unit 8

An Early Bird or a Night Owl?

Lead-in

1 **Read the sentences and circle the correct answers.**

1 The man in the picture is Bob Ellis. He is a ...*Night Owl*...
   a) shark trainer   **b)** dolphin trainer

2 Bob works at a(n) ....
   a) swimming-pool **b)** aquarium

3 Bob usually ....
   a) cleans the aquarium
   b) feeds and trains the dolphins

4 His job is ....
   a) tiring   **b)** boring

5 An early bird is someone who ....
   a) gets up early   **b)** gets up late

6 An owl is a bird which sleeps ....
   a) during the day **b)** during the night

2 ▣ **Read the sentences about Bob Ellis, then listen and write T (for true) or F (for false).**

1 "I like my job a lot."   ....
2 "I work long hours."   ....
3 His day starts at six o'clock in the morning.   ....
4 He catches the train to work.   ....
5 In the evening, Bob usually watches TV.   ....
6 He loves going for long walks in the countryside.   ....

Reading

3 **Read the text and answer the questions. Then, explain the words in bold.**

1 Does Bob like his job? Why (not)?
2 Why is his job tiring?
3 What does Bob do in the morning/afternoon/evening?
4 What does Bob do in his free time?
5 How does Bob feel about his life?
6 What tense do we use to describe daily routines?

Around the Clock with Bob Ellis

Bob Ellis, 29, is a dolphin trainer. "I like my job a lot because I love working with animals. It is tiring though, as I work **long hours**," he says.

Bob is an early bird. His day starts at five o'clock in the morning. He gets up, has a shower, and then he gets dressed. After breakfast, at about six o'clock, he catches the bus to work. He arrives at the aquarium at half past six and feeds the dolphins. After that, they **practise** for the show until lunch-time. Bob has a **break** for lunch from half past twelve till half past one, then the show starts. At five o'clock in the afternoon, he feeds the dolphins again and then he goes home. In the evening, Bob usually watches TV. He doesn't go out very often **during** the week because he goes to bed **early**.

And what does Bob do in his free time? He loves going for **long walks** in the **countryside** with his dog, Jack. Bob also likes swimming at the pool, but he never swims in the sea because he's **afraid of** sharks!

"I **feel** very **satisfied** with my life at the moment," says Bob. "I've got a great job and I enjoy my free time. Who could ask for more?"

• Vocabulary

4 **Choose words from the list to fill in the gaps, then use them to make sentences.**

an early, gets, has, arrives, long, a night, free, goes to, goes, watches, catches, afraid of

1 ....long..........walks
2 ....an early...... bird
3 ....a night........owl
4 He .... a shower.
5 He ..has... dressed.
6 He .... the bus.
7 He ......gets.... home.
8 He is at the aquarium.
9 He ...watches... TV.
10 He goes to.. bed early.
11 He arrives at time
12 He is afraid of sharks.

• Speaking

Read the text again and make notes under the following headings. Close your books, look at your notes and talk about Bob's daily routine and free-time activities. Start like this: *Bob is a dolphin trainer. He gets up at five o'clock in the morning...*

Bob's job:
What Bob does: in the morning - in the afternoon - in the evening - in his free time

Language Development

• Telling the Time

We tell the time in two different ways.

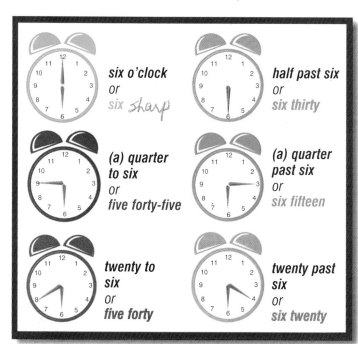

six o'clock
or
six *sharp*

half past six
or
six thirty

(a) quarter
to six
or
five forty-five

(a) quarter
past six
or
six fifteen

twenty to
six
or
five forty

twenty past
six
or
six twenty

5 **Look at the clock faces, then, in pairs, ask and answer questions, as in the example. Tell the time in both ways, as explained in the theory box.**

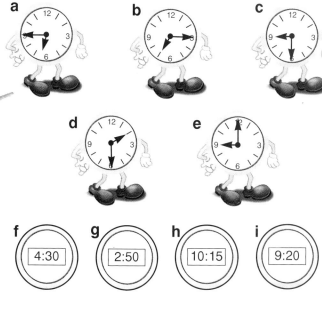

a **b** **c**

d **e**

f 4:30 **g** 2:50 **h** 10:15 **i** 9:20

SA: *What time is it?*
SB: *It's (a) quarter to seven.*

SA: *What's the time?*
SB: *It's six forty-five.*

it's (a) 11 Past five
it (a) thirty Past nine
seven

It' eleven fourteen
it's nine thirty

6 **Ask and answer questions, as in the examples.**

S1: *What time does the plane from Tokyo arrive?*
S2: *It arrives at (a) quarter past five. What time ...*

	ARRIVALS				
	Flight No.	Origin	Time of Arrival	Status	Gate
	UN 908	Tokyo	5:15	on time	A4
	SW 575	Brussels	5:30	on time	A1
	NW 202	Montreal	6:45	on time	B6
	SA 117	Cairo	7:00	on time	B3

S1: *What time does the plane for New York leave?*
S2: *It leaves at twenty past seven. What time ...*

	DEPARTURES			
	Flight No.	Destination	Time of Departure	Status	Gate
	TWA 806	New York	7:20	now boarding	B6
	KLM 772	Amsterdam	8:10	now boarding	C5
	EA 201	Tel Aviv	8:15	now boarding	C1
	AF 550	Paris	8:45	now boarding	B4

• Reading & Listening

7 🔊 **Read the text, then listen and fill in the missing times. Read the text again and answer the following questions.**

1 What time do shops close on Saturday?
2 What time do banks close on Tuesday?
3 Which day do post offices open from 8:30 until noon?
4 What time do chemists open on Tuesday?
5 What time do restaurants open for dinner?
6 Are there any restaurants in Holland which stay open late?

Welcome to Holland

Shops

Shops are open Monday to Friday from 9 am until **a)** .... pm, and on Saturday from 9 am until 4 or **b)** .... pm. Many places have late-night shopping on Thursday or Friday evenings.

Banks and Post Offices

Banks are open Monday to Friday from **c)** ....am until 5 pm and sometimes later on Thursday or Friday. Post offices are open Monday to Friday from 8:30 am until **d)** ...... pm, and often on Saturday from 8:30 am until noon.

Chemists

Chemists are open Monday to Friday from 8 am until **e)** .... pm. Some chemists stay open to cover evenings, nights and weekends.

Restaurants

Restaurants are generally open for lunch from **f)** ....am until 3 pm and for dinner from **g)** .... until 10 pm. The Dutch are not late diners, but there are some restaurants which stay open late in the big cities.

Writing (Project)

Write a text similar to the one in Ex. 7 about the opening hours of shops and restaurants in your country.

8 **a) Label the pictures with the adjectives in the list.**
happy, tired, stressed, satisfied, bored
b) Match the adjectives to the reasons. Make sentences joining them with *because*, as in the example.

*I feel happy **because** I enjoy my work.*

happy	I work long hours.
stressed	I enjoy my work.
bored	I earn a lot of money.
satisfied	I talk to angry customers.
tired	I do the same things every day.

9 Read the text about Kim's daily routine and fill in the gaps using phrases from the list. Some of the phrases do not match any of the pictures.

catch the bus, get up, have a shower, have breakfast/lunch/dinner, watch TV, go to bed, do her homework, get dressed, leave home, finish work, read a book, go to work, go dancing

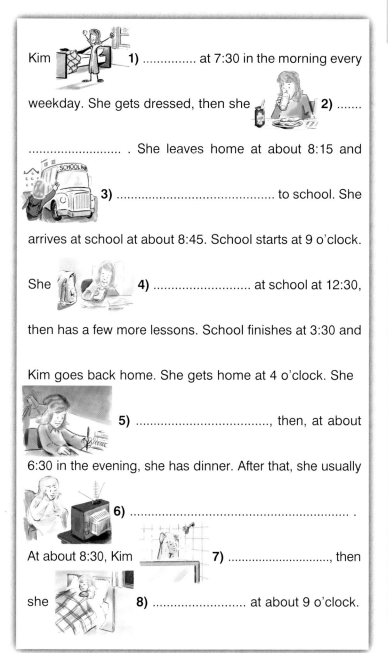

Kim **1)** .... at 7:30 in the morning every weekday. She gets dressed, then she **2)** ....

.... She leaves home at about 8:15 and

3) .... to school. She

arrives at school at about 8:45. School starts at 9 o'clock.

She **4)** .... at school at 12:30,

then has a few more lessons. School finishes at 3:30 and

Kim goes back home. She gets home at 4 o'clock. She

5) ...., then, at about

6:30 in the evening, she has dinner. After that, she usually

6) ....

At about 8:30, Kim **7)** ...., then

she **8)** .... at about 9 o'clock.

● Speaking

10 Choose phrases from Ex. 9 and talk about your daily routine. What do you do in the *morning/afternoon/evening*?

● Grammar: Adverbs of Frequency

11 Study the examples, then underline the correct words to complete the rule.

*I **usually** get up at half past seven in the morning. I am **never** late for school.*

Adverbs of frequency usually come **before/after** the main verb, but **before/after** the verb *"to be"*. They tell us how often something happens.

12 a) Listen and tick the boxes. Then, make sentences, as in the example.

*Laura **never** goes climbing on Sundays.*

	never 0%	rarely 10%	sometimes 25%	often 50%	usually 75%	always 100%
go climbing						
wash the car						
go to the gym						
cook						
go on a picnic						
go dancing						

b) Talk about yourself. What do you *never/rarely/sometimes/often/usually/always* do on Sundays? Choose phrases from the list below. You can add some of your own ideas.

do the washing-up, go jogging, go to the cinema, go shopping, eat out, watch TV, go fishing, visit museums, go climbing, go windsurfing, meet friends

37

● **Speaking**

13 In pairs, ask and answer questions, as in the example. Then, write a short paragraph about your partner.

How often do you...

go to the swimming-pool?
go to the theatre?
clean your room?
go fishing?
go out with your family?
play computer games?
watch TV?
meet your friends?
go shopping?

> **never**
> **every day/month/**
> **evening, etc**
> **every two/three**
> **days/Sunday, etc**
> **sometimes**
> **once/twice a week/**
> **month, etc**

SA: How often do you go to the swimming-pool?
SB: Twice a week.
SA: How often do you go to the theatre?
SB: Never...
Tony goes to the swimming-pool twice a week, but he never goes to the theatre. ...

14 Number the months in the correct order.
🔊 Now listen and repeat.

..1.. January | ..... July | ..... October | ..... June

..... April | ..... November | ..... August | ..... February

..... May | ..... September | ..... March | ..... December

● **Grammar:** Prepositions of Time

15 Study the rules, then fill in *on, in* and *at*.

....	....	....
six o'clock the weekend night noon	Friday(s) Sunday morning(s) 2 August 6 May, 1978	May spring/summer, etc the morning/ evening/afternoon 1998

We use **at** with the time and with *the weekend, night* and *noon.*
We use **on** with days of the week, the parts of a particular day and dates.
We use **in** with months, seasons, years· and with *the morning/evening/afternoon.*

16 🔊 Study the table, then listen and fill in the missing information. Next, make sentences, as in the example. Finally, write about yourself.

	DATE	MONTH	YEAR	TIME	PART OF DAY
Tom	Friday 22nd	March	1957	10:30	night
Mary	Monday 6th	July	....	2:00	....
Roy	.... 3rd	August	1955	....	afternoon
You					

*Tom was born **on** Friday the 22nd of March, **in** 1957, **at** half past ten **at** night.*

17 Fill in *at, in* or *on* then talk about Henry's daily routine and free-time activities.

Henry Jones, 50, is a farmer. "It's a tiring job," he says, "but I like it a lot."

Every day, Henry wakes up **1)** .... half past four **2)** .... the morning and milks the cows. He finishes **3)** .... about half past six. After that, he goes back to the farmhouse and has breakfast, then he feeds the animals. He has lunch **4)** .... noon. **5)** .... two o'clock, he goes to the fields and works there until five. **6)** .... the evening, he milks the cows again, then he goes back home and has a shower. He sometimes watches TV before he goes to bed **7)** .... about nine.

8) .... Saturday afternoons, he goes to the local playing-field to watch the village team play football. Henry likes football a lot. **9)** .... Sundays, Henry relaxes. "I like the way I live," says Henry. "Working in the open air makes me feel good."

Pronunciation

18 🔊 **Listen and tick. Listen again and repeat.**

	/ θ /	/ ð /
this		
three		
bath		

	/ θ /	/ ð /
father		
both		
then		

• Communication: Telling the Time

19 🔊 **Fill in the gaps, then listen and check. Finally, in pairs, act out similar dialogues.**

A: Excuse me, ... the time?
B: Sorry?
A: What .... is it?
B: It's a quarter .... eight.
A: Thanks.

• Interviewing a Celebrity

20 **a) Read the dialogue and complete the questions.**
🔊 **b) Listen and check your answers.**
c) What's Annie's daily routine?
d) In pairs, read out the dialogue.

P: Our special guest in the studio today is our local singer, Annie Franklyn. Welcome to the show, Annie.
A: Thanks. It's great to be here.
P: Well Annie, **1)** .... your job?
A: Yes, I like it a lot. The only bad thing is that I don't see my family and friends very often. I'm very busy.
P: Well, tell us about a typical day in your life. **2)** ....
.... do you get up?
A: I usually get up at noon because I go to bed very late every night. I have lunch at about two.
P: **3)** What .... then?
A: I go to the club to practise for about two hours, then I go home or sometimes I go shopping. I go back to the club again at about eight o'clock in the evening.
P: **4)** .... the show start?
A: At ten o'clock, and we don't usually finish until two o'clock in the morning.
P: **5)** .... then?
A: I go back home, read for a while, then go to bed.
P: Annie, I know you don't have much free time, but **6)** .... doing in your free time?
A: I love going to the cinema or having dinner with friends. I don't really like going to parties, though.
P: One last question. **7)** .... satisfied with your life?
A: Oh yes. I love singing and I enjoy my free time.
P: Annie Franklyn, thank you for joining us.

• Vocabulary Revision Game

21 **Work in two teams. Take it in turns to choose words from the list and make sentences. Each correct sentence gets one point. The team with the most points is the winner.**

feed, catch the bus, aquarium, in the afternoon, go dancing, go out with your family, get up, (a) quarter to, go to bed, half past, rarely, milk the cows, often, relax, always, meet my friends, satisfied

Writing (an article about a celebrity's daily routine)

Use the plan below and the information from Ex. 20, as well as the picture from the Photo File section, to write an article about Annie Franklyn. Use the text in Ex.3 as a model.

Plan

Para 1: name, job, feelings about the job
↓
Para 2: daily routine (what she does in the morning/afternoon/evening/at night)
↓
Para 3: free-time activities (what she likes/doesn't like doing)
↓
Para 4: how she feels about her life

Words of Wisdom

Read the sentences. What do they mean?

* The early bird catches the worm.
* Early to bed and early to rise, makes a man healthy, wealthy and wise.

UNIT 6

Birds of a Feather...

Lead-in

1 Look at the pictures and match them to the animals in the list.

dolphin, lion, parrot, penguins

Which of them are ...

○ birds?   ○ mammals?

Which of them have ...

○ fur?   ○ fins?   ○ a tail?   ○ skin?
○ feathers?   ○ wings?   ○ a mane?
○ legs?

Which of them can ...

○ fly?   ○ run?   ○ swim?

2 📼 First, read these sentences, then listen and mark them as T (true) or F (false).

1 Dolphins are mammals.   ......
2 Dolphins live in water.   ......
3 Dolphins have got grey fur.   ......
4 Dolphins eat fish.   ......
5 Penguins haven't got wings.   ......
6 Penguins can fly.   ......
7 Penguins live in Antarctica.   ......
8 Penguins live for about ten years.   ......

Reading

3 Read the texts about dolphins and penguins and:
a) find *three* ways that dolphins are like penguins;
b) explain the words in bold.

Dolphins are mammals. They have babies and feed them on milk. Dolphins are not fish, but they live in water. They can swim very well. They haven't got legs. They've got grey skin and a big **smile**. They've also got fins and a tail to help them swim. They **weigh** from seventy to five hundred kilos.

Dolphins are very **intelligent** animals. They can **easily** learn how to play games and are **friendly** to people.

Dolphins live in **warm seas** in many different **parts of the world**. They live in small **groups** and they eat fish. They live for about fifty years.

Penguins **lay eggs** and they've got wings, so they are like other birds, but they can't fly! They can swim very well, though. They are black and white, and they've got small wings, very short legs and a short tail. They've also got **thick** feathers to keep them **warm** in **cold water**. They weigh about twenty kilos.

Penguins look **funny** when they walk. However, when they are in the water, they swim like fish.

Penguins live on the **ice** of Antarctica and in the sea around it. They live in big groups and they eat fish. They live for about twenty years.

c) Read the texts again, and answer the questions.

1 What can dolphins do very well?
2 Where do dolphins live?
3 How long do dolphins live?
4 Why are penguins unusual birds?
5 What have penguins got to keep them warm?
6 What do penguins eat?

40

• Speaking

Read the texts again, then copy and complete the table. Finally, talk about each animal.

	DOLPHINS	PENGUINS
kind of animal:	mammals	
unusual because:		
they can:		
they've got:		
they weigh:		
they live:		
they eat:		
they live for:		

Dolphins are mammals. ...

Language Development

• Vocabulary

4 a) **Match the names of the animals to the pictures. Close your books and say the names of as many animals as you can remember.**

a. crocodile, *b.* butterfly, *c.* monkey, *d.* horse, *e.* rooster, *f.* snake, *g.* cow, *h.* dog, *i.* cat

1 ...a...   2 ....   3 ....

4 ....   5 ....   6 ....

7 ....   8 ....   9 ....

b) **Which of these animals are *reptiles/mammals/ insects/birds*?**

Crocodiles are reptiles.

5 **Read the list of words below, then label the parts of the animals' bodies. What are the names of these animals?**

paws, feathers, fur, tail, beak, ears

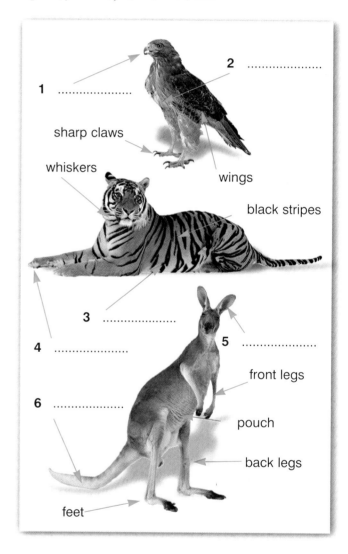

1 ....
2 ....
sharp claws
whiskers
wings
black stripes
3 ....
4 ....
5 ....
6 ....
front legs
pouch
back legs
feet

6 **Choose words from the list to fill in the gaps, then use them to make sentences.**

lay, short, intelligent, keep, have, big, warm, look, parts, thick

1 .... animals	6 .... of the world
2 .... feathers	7 to .... them warm
3 a .... tail	8 to .... funny
4 a .... smile	9 to .... eggs
5 in .... seas	10 to .... babies

7 Fill in the missing prepositions.

1 Dolphins feed their babies .... milk.
2 They weigh .... 70 .... 500 kilos.
3 Dolphins are friendly .... people.
4 They live .... warm seas.
5 They live .... about fifty years.
6 Penguins live .... the ice .... Antarctica.
7 They live .... big groups.

8 Listen to the animal noises and tick (✓) the animals you can hear. Which of them are *wild animals* and which are *farm animals*? Finally, write sentences as in the example.

I can hear a hen. Hens are farm animals.
I can't hear a crocodile. Crocodiles are wild animals.

a hen	✓	a crocodile	☐	a horse	☐	a monkey	☐
a lion	☐	a tiger	☐	a parrot	☐	a kangaroo	☐
a cow	☐	a snake	☐	a sheep	☐	a penguin	☐

9 Read the text about koalas and underline the correct word. Then, answer the questions.

1 What can koalas do?
2 What do they look like?
3 Where do they live?
4 How long do they live?

Koalas are 1) **mammals/fish** and, like dolphins, they have babies and feed them on 2) **water/milk**. Mothers carry their young in a small pouch for the first six months of their lives. Koalas can 3) **fly/climb** very well. They can swim very well, too. They have got thick, 4) **grey/black** fur and a big, black nose. They've also got very sharp 5) **paws/claws**. Koalas live and sleep in the tops of eucalyptus trees in eastern 6)**Australia/America**. They live alone and eat eucalyptus leaves. Koalas live for about 7) **fifteen/fifty** years.

10 Write the names of these animals and their young under the pictures. Then, make sentences as in the example.

cat, chicks, dog, ducklings, duck, kittens, puppies, hen

1 ...cat...   2 ...kittens...   3 ....   4 ....

5 ....   6 ....   7 ....   8 ....

A cat has kittens.

Quiz

11 First, read the statements and mark them as T (true) or F (false).
Then, listen and check your answers.

1 Snakes can't hear. ...T... ....
2 Dolphins are about 1-4 metres long. ....
3 Snakes lay eggs. ....
4 Chimpanzees weigh 45-80 kilos. ....
5 Lions sleep for 5 hours a day. ....
6 Sea lions live in small groups. ....
7 Penguins' eggs are black. ....
8 Eagles can't see well. ....
9 Elephants can live for about 60 years. ....
10 Penguins can be under the water for 18 minutes. ....

• Grammar: Question Words

12 **Look at the questions and match them to the answers.**

WHAT is this animal?	- On the plains in Africa and India.
WHERE does it live?	- About 3.3 metres.
WHEN does it sleep?	- An elephant.
WHY can it walk long distances?	- At night.
HOW long is its trunk?	- Four.
HOW tall is it?	- Because it has got strong legs.
HOW much does it weigh?	- About 3.1 metres.
HOW many legs has it got?	- About 60 years.
HOW long does it live?	- About 4,000 kilos.

13 **Read the text, then, in pairs, ask and answer questions, as in the table above.**

SA: What is this animal?
SB: It's a kangaroo. ...

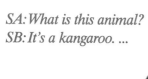

Kangaroos are mammals. They have babies and feed them on milk. They live in Australia. They are about two metres tall and weigh about sixty kilos. Kangaroos have got two back legs, two short front legs and a long tail. They can jump very high because their back legs are very strong. They sleep during the day and they eat leaves. Kangaroos carry their babies in a pouch. They live in small groups. They live for about fifteen to twenty years.

Writing (Project)

Look at the pictures and the information about these animals and ask and answer questions, as in the example. Then, write fact files about tigers and sea lions. Use the text in Ex. 13 as a model. Decorate your project with pictures from the Photo File section.

*S1: **What is** this animal?*
*S2: It's a tiger. **How much does it** weigh?*
*S3: It weighs about 200 kilos. **What does it** eat?...*

...this animal?	tiger
...weigh?	about 200 kilos
...eat?	deer and monkeys
...sleep?	during the day
...live?	forests in India
...live?	about 15 years

...this animal?	sea lion
...weigh?	about 250 kilos
...eat?	fish
...can/do?	swim very well
...live?	the Pacific Ocean
...live?	about 15 years

• Speaking

14 Study the colours and sizes, then read the examples. Finally, in pairs, ask and answer questions about the animals, as in the example.

Colours

brown white grey pink green

yellow black blue purple red

Sizes

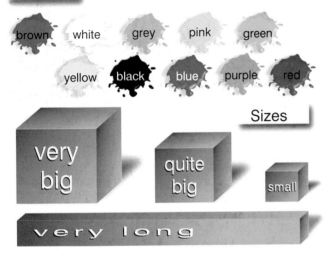

very big

quite big

small

very long

quite long

short quite short

What is this animal?	It's a cow.
What colour is it?	It's brown.
How big is it?	It's very big.
How long are its ears?	They're quite short.
How long is its tail?	It's very long.

A
B
C
D

• Grammar: Irregular Nouns

15 Fill in the table with words from the list.

deer, fish, goose, mice, oxen, sheep

SINGULAR	PLURAL
....	geese
mouse	....
ox	....
....	sheep
deer	....
....	fish

What are the plurals of these words?

man .... child ....
woman .... person ....

• Speaking

16 In pairs, ask and answer questions about the animals below, as in the example.

SA: What is this animal?
SB: It's a mouse. Have mice got wings?
SA: No, mice haven't got wings.

1 have/got wings?
2 can/run?
3 have/got short legs?

4 have/got whiskers?
5 can/fly?
6 have/got fur?

• Vocabulary Revision Game

17 Work in two teams. Take it in turns to choose words from the list and make sentences. Each correct sentence gets one point. The team with the most points is the winner.

fur, skin, wings, weigh, intelligent, feathers, what, pouch, reptiles, mammals, insects, paws, feed, where, sharp claws, trunk, whiskers, how big, how long

18 *Rose has got two pet rabbits and her friend Ron is asking her questions about them.* Match Ron's questions to Rose's answers, then act out the dialogue.

1	What are their names? **B (Hansel and Gretel.)**
2	How old are they?
3	What do they eat?
4	When do you feed them?
5	Where do they live?
6	How often do you clean it?

A Lettuce and carrots.
B Hansel and Gretel.
C One year old.
D In a big cage.
E Two or three times a week.
F Every morning.

Pronunciation

19 📼 Listen and tick. Listen again and repeat.

	/ ɛ /	/ ɜː /
bed		
bird		
herd		

	/ ɛ /	/ ɜː /
head		
ten		
turn		

• Communication: Asking about Pets

20 📼 Read the dialogue, then listen and fill in the missing words. Close your books and, in pairs, act out the dialogue.

Tom: .... your dog's name?
Sally: Lady.
Tom: What .... of dog is it?
Sally: It's a collie.
Tom: Is it a male or a female?
Sally: It's a ....
Tom: .... is she?
Sally: She's .... old.

21 📼 Read the table, then listen and fill in the gaps. Finally, look at your notes and talk about each animal.

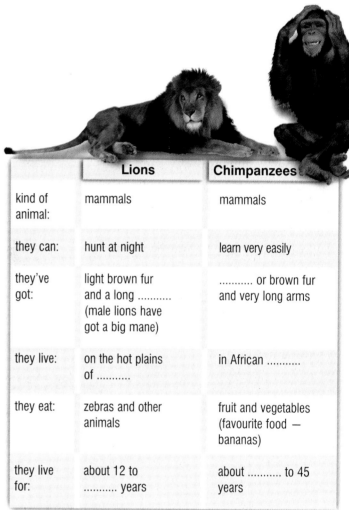

	Lions	Chimpanzees
kind of animal:	mammals	mammals
they can:	hunt at night	learn very easily
they've got:	light brown fur and a long .... (male lions have got a big mane)	.... or brown fur and very long arms
they live:	on the hot plains of	in African ....
they eat:	zebras and other animals	fruit and vegetables (favourite food — bananas)
they live for:	about 12 to .... years	about .... to 45 years

Writing (descriptions of animals)

Your teacher has asked you to write two short texts (50 - 80 words each) about *lions* and *chimpanzees*. Use the information from Ex. 21 and the pictures from the Photo File section to write about these wild animals. Use the texts in Ex. 3 as models.

Words of Wisdom

Read these sentences. What do they mean?

- Birds of a feather flock together.
- While the cat's away, the mice will play.
- Big fish eat little fish.
- Curiosity killed the cat.

The Loch Ness Monster

1 Look at the pictures on p. 46 and answer the questions.

1 Where is Sandra in the first picture?
2 Who saves Sandra?
3 How does Sandra feel in the third picture?
4 What is in the envelope?
5 Whose face is it in the photographs?

2 📼 Listen to the episode. Who says the following? Write D for David, S for Sandra or M for Mike.

1 "I'm scared!" ....
2 "Just take my hand!" ....
3 "We're safe now." ....
4 "That's interesting!" ....

3 Fill in the opposites: *big*, *short*, or *warm*.

1 cold ≠ ....   3 small ≠...........
2 long ≠ ....

4 Read the episode and mark the correct sentences with *Yes* and the incorrect ones with *No*. Then, make sentences as in the example.

No, it hasn't. The monster has got a small head.

1 The monster has got a big head. ...*No*...
2 The water is warm. ....
3 The monster's name is Nessie. ....
4 The monster has got a short neck. ....

Loch Ness

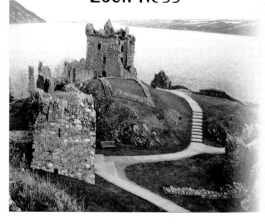

5 The adjectives in the list describe how each person feels. Label the pictures with the correct adjectives. Then, say how David, Sandra and Mike feel in each picture.

scared, surprised, tired, angry, happy, upset

a. Mike is surprised.

a ...*surprised*...
b ....
c ....
d ....
e ....
f ....

6 a) Read the episode and find *seven imperatives* and *six questions*.
📼 **b) Listen and follow the episode on p. 46. Finally, act out the episode.**

7 This is a summary of the two episodes. There are four mistakes in it. Read the text, find the mistakes and correct them.

In the offices of The Morning Sun, Mike, the editor, asks David and Sandra to write a story about the Loch Ness monster. David and Sandra go to the loch by bus. They hire a boat. David sees the monster and takes photographs of it. The monster is small. Sandra falls into the water and David saves her. David telephones Mike and tells him about the accident. Mike is happy because he thinks they have got photographs of the monster. Unfortunately, there is no monster in the photographs. They are all photographs of David's face.

8 Read the short text and fill in the gaps with words from the list. What is the name of the castle?

lake, monster, long, dark, trees, visit

Loch Ness is a big lake in Scotland. It is in the Scottish Highlands. It is twenty-three miles 1) .... and one mile wide. It's a very deep 2) .... The water is 3) .... and cold. People believe that a 4) .... lives in the waters of Loch Ness. They call this monster Nessie. There are many stories from people about Nessie. There are lots of 5) .... by the lake. There is also a castle called Urquhart Castle. A lot of tourists 6) .... Loch Ness every year. They all hope to see Nessie.

UNIT 7

Come Rain or Shine

Lead-in

1 In which card is the weather ...

1 cold, cloudy and windy?
2 freezing cold and snowy?
3 hot and sunny?
4 warm and sunny?

2 Label the cards with the names of the seasons: *summer, winter, spring* or *autumn*. Then, ask and answer questions, as in the example.

S1: What's the weather like in spring?
S2: It's warm and sunny in spring.

3 Match these sentences to the cards. Two of them do not match any of the cards.

1 There are **clouds** in the sky and the wind is **blowing**. It's **cloudy** and windy. ☐
2 The sun is **shining**. It's sunny. ☐
3 It is **raining**. It's a **rainy** day. ☐
4 It is **snowing**. It's a **snowy** day. ☐
5 There is a lot of **fog**. It's **foggy**. ☐

4 Look at the cards. Which card shows someone who is wearing:

1 a red coat? **2** gloves? **3** boots? **4** a pink dress? **5** a heavy jacket? **6** a blue hat? **7** a swimming-costume? **8** a jacket and a red tie? **9** a black cap?

5 Match the cards to the sentences below.

1 ☐	They are sitting on the beach under a sunshade.
2 ☐	They are throwing snowballs.
3 ☐	They are picking flowers.
4 ☐	They are walking by the lake.

6 📼 Listen and match the weather to the places.

1 It is snowing heavily today.   **a** ☐ Sydney
2 It's very hot and the sun is shining.   **b** ☐ London
3 It's windy today and it is raining.   **c** ☐ Warsaw

48

Reading

7 **Read these postcards and underline the sentences which describe the people's clothes in each picture. Then, answer the questions.**

1 What is the weather like in Warsaw, London and Sydney?
2 What are Tom's children doing?
3 What are Tracy's children doing?
4 What are Pamela's family doing?

A

Dear Sally,

A Happy New Year to all of you. You can't imagine how cold it is in Warsaw! It is snowing heavily today, so the children are wearing their heavy jackets and gloves to keep them warm. They are making a snowman in the park at the moment.
Hope to see you soon.

Best wishes,

Tom

Sally Jones
12 Swan St
London SW1 4GB
England

B

Dear Mum and Dad,

Greetings from London. It's windy today and it is raining. The children are in their pyjamas in the living-room. They are very happy as they are decorating the Christmas tree at the moment.
We miss you a lot.

Love,
Tracy

Mr & Mrs Johnson
2 Via Torino
Rome
Italy

C

Dear Aunt Bessie,

Season's greetings from Sydney. The weather is fantastic today and we are on the beach. It's very hot and the sun is shining, so we are all in our swimming costumes. Mum, Dad, Sheila and Frank are making a sandcastle. There are a lot of people on the beach today. Everyone is swimming and enjoying the good weather.
Come and see us soon!

Lots of love,
Pamela

Mrs Bessie Bates
27 Park Lane
London SW3 9RY
England

• Speaking

Read the postcards again and make notes about each under these headings: *city-weather-clothes-activities.* **Then, look at your notes and talk about each person, as in the example.** *Tom is in Warsaw. It's very cold there and it is snowing ...*

Language Development

• Vocabulary

8 **Choose words from the list to fill in the gaps, then use them to make sentences.**

miss, keep, make, season's, heavy, decorate, enjoy

1 to............................ the Christmas tree
2 We .... you a lot.
3 to .... the good weather
4 .... greetings
5 .... jackets
6 to .... a snowman
7 to .... them warm

9 **Fill in** *on, in, at, of* **or** *from.*

1 .... Warsaw; **2** .... the park; **3** .... the moment;
4 Greetings .... London; **5** .... their pyjamas;
6 .... the beach; **7** Lots .... love

10 **Look at today's international weather chart. Ask and answer questions, as in the example.**

S1: *What's the weather like in Cairo today?*
S2: *It's warm and sunny.*
S1: *What's the temperature in Cairo today?*
S2: *It's 25°C./ It's 77°F.*

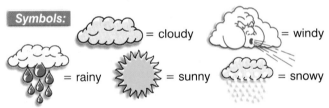

Symbols:

= cloudy
= windy
= rainy
= sunny
= snowy

freezing cold	cold	chilly	cool	warm	hot	boiling hot

-5°C/23°F 5°C/41°F 10°C/50°F 15°C/59°F 25°C/77°F 30°C/86°F 35°C/95°F

• °C: degrees Celsius   • °F: degrees Fahrenheit

		C	F			C	F
Cairo		25	77	**Paris**		5	41
London		10	50	**Prague**		-5	23
Madrid		5	41	**Rome**		15	59
Manila		30	86	**Singapore**		35	95

• Speaking

11 **Which of the activities in the list can you do when it is:** *snowy? hot and sunny? cold and rainy?*
go to the beach, make a snowman, go on a picnic, watch TV, go swimming, sunbathe, read a book, ski
When it is snowy you can ski or make a snowman.

• Grammar: Present Continuous

12 **Study the table, then complete the rule.**

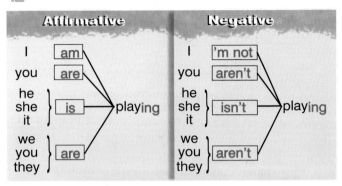

Affirmative	Negative
I **am**	I **'m not**
you **are**	you **aren't**
he she it **is** ⟩playing	he she it **isn't** ⟩playing
we you they **are**	we you they **aren't**

To form the present continuous we use the verb "**to be**" and add .... to the base form of the main verb. We use the present continuous for actions happening **now, at the moment of speaking**. We use this tense with ***now, at present*** and ***at the moment***.
She**'s playing** football **now**.
She **isn't eating** an ice-cream **at the moment**.

13 **Read the texts in Ex. 7 again and fill in the *-ing* form of the verbs in the table below, then complete the rules.**

Spelling			
snow	....	sw**im**	....
wear	....	mak**e**	....
rain	....	decorat**e**	....
enjoy	....	shin**e**	....

- **Most verbs** take **-ing** after the base form of the main verb.
- **Verbs ending in one stressed vowel and a consonant** double the **consonant** and take ....
- **Verbs ending in -e** drop the **e** and take ....

14 **Complete the short answers in this table.**

Interrogative			Short answers
Am	I	playing?	Yes, I am./No, I'm not.
Are	you		Yes, you are./. No, ...
Is	he she it	playing?	Yes, ... /No, he isn't. Yes, she is./No, ... Yes, it is./No, ...
Are	we you they	playing?	Yes, .../No, we aren't. Yes, you are./No, ... Yes, they are./No, ...

15 Look at the picture and correct the sentences, as in the example.

1 Patty is swimming.
Wrong! Patty isn't swimming. She's sunbathing.
2 Sue and Molly are playing tennis.
3 Ann is sleeping.
4 Tony is listening to music.
5 Jim and Ian are reading a book.

16 First, listen to the sounds and tick (✓) what you hear, then ask and answer questions, as in the example.

S1: Is Tony watching TV?
S2: No, he isn't. He's playing tennis.

1	**Tony:** watch TV	☐	play tennis	✓
2	**Stella:** drive a car	☐	have a shower	☐
3	**Bob & Keith:** swim	☐	sleep	☐
4	**They:** listen to music	☐	play computer games	☐
5	**James:** ride a horse	☐	ride a motorbike	☐
6	**She:** play the guitar	☐	play the piano	☐
7	**They:** walk	☐	run	☐

• Reading & Listening

17 a) Listen to the weather descriptions and match them to the pictures.
b) Read the texts and say which season each person likes most, and why. Finally, talk about the seasons in your country.

1

2

3

A
"In Britain the weather is often rainy, but in winter it's also very cold and windy. In autumn and spring it can be quite windy but it's not very cold. Summer can be quite warm but it can also be cloudy. I like spring a lot because the trees are green and there are lots of flowers. I often go for walks in the park, then. "
Karen

B
"Brazil has a warm climate. The winter isn't very cold. In spring and autumn it is warm, but rainy. In summer it's nearly always hot and sunny. Sometimes, it rains suddenly and then the sun comes out again! Summer is my favourite season. I love swimming and sunbathing at the beach. We have lots of fun there."
Miguel

C
"In Finland the weather is very cold in the winter and very warm in the summer. The winter is very long and there are days when the sun doesn't appear at all. The summer is short, but it's warm, because the days are so long. The sun shines all day and night for most of the summer. I like winter the best because there is always snow and I often go skiing."
Anita

Writing (Project)

Write a short paragraph about the different seasons in your country. Write which is your favourite season and what you like doing then. Use the texts in Ex. 17 as models.

18 a) Look at the pictures and the names of the clothes. Use words from the list to fill in the gaps.

hat, shorts, tie, trousers, skirt, blouse

b) 🎞 **Listen and number the pictures as the designer describes each one. Then, look at the pictures and describe each person's clothes.**

shirt

jumper

c ....

dress

e ....

jacket

cap

T-shirt

a ....

socks

suit

f ....

boots

trainers

tights

Jenny

Paul

Lucy

T-shirt

shirt

b ....

T-shirt

jacket

d ....

Diana

John

jeans

1 **Steve**

shoes

sandals

Mary

• Game

19 Choose a student in your class and describe his/her clothes. The first person to guess who you are describing goes next.

Pronunciation

20 🎞 **Listen and tick. Listen again and repeat.**

	/ n /	/ ŋ /
wearing		
rain		
making		
shine		
fishing		
run		

• Speaking

21 Look at the pictures, then read the dialogue. In pairs, act out similar dialogues, using the prompts below and the words in the pictures.

dress, skirt, jumper, shirt, shoes, suit

TOO...

tight

small

short

expensive

big

long

*SA: What do you think of this **skirt**?*
*SB: Well, I think it's **too short**.*
*SA: What about these **shoes**?*
*SB: Oh no! They're **too expensive**.*

● Grammar: Present Simple vs Present Continuous

22 **Study the examples, then complete the rules.**

!

*John usually **wears** jeans and T-shirts.*
*John**'s wearing** a suit and tie today.*

We use .... to talk about habits and daily routines.
We use .... to talk about actions happening now, at the moment of speaking.

23 🔊 **Listen to the dialogue and repeat. Then, use the prompts to act out similar dialogues.**

Look at Pam! She's wearing a dress today!

Oh, yes! She usually wears jeans and T-shirts. She looks nice in a dress!

- John / shirt and tie / jumpers
- Ellen / shorts / long skirts
- Tim / jeans and trainers / a suit
- Donna / trousers / dresses

● Vocabulary Revision Game

24 **Work in two teams. Take it in turns to choose words from the list and make sentences. Each correct sentence gets one point. The team with the most points is the winner.**

jacket, snowy, boiling hot, what about, hot, enjoy, freezing cold, weather, cloudy, too tight, too long, sunbathing, temperature, season

Communication: Buying Clothes

25 🔊 **Read the dialogue and fill in the gaps. Then, listen and check. Finally, act out similar dialogues about the other clothes you can see in the pictures.**

A: **1)** .... I help you?
B: Yes, **2)** .... I'm looking for a jumper.
A: What colour **3)** .... you like?
B: Yellow.
A: **4)** .... you are.
B: Can I try it on, please?
A: Yes, of course.

Writing (a postcard)

Use the plan below to write a postcard to a friend (40-60 words). Use the postcards in Ex.7 as models.

Plan

Dear + (your friend's first name)

    Greetings from ...
- Say where you are
- Say what the weather is like
- Say what clothes you are wearing
- Say what you are doing now
    See you soon.

            Lots of love,
            (your first name)

Words of Wisdom

Read these sentences. What do they mean?

- Come rain or shine.
- March comes in like a lion and goes out like a lamb.
- Clothes make the man.

Enjoy your Meal

wine

pear

pineapple

coffee

beer

cherries

strawberries

coconut

orange juice

milk

bananas

water

tea

orange

grapes

apple

Lead-in

1 **Look at the pictures and answer the questions below.**

a Which of the foods/drinks do you like/not like?

b Which are vegetables/meat/fruit/sweets?

c When do you eat breakfast/lunch/dinner?

d How often do you eat fruit/sweets/vegetables/meat?

e Which of the foods/drinks can you have for breakfast/dessert/a light meal /a traditional English breakfast?

pepper

tomatoes

lettuce

salad

chocolate cake

ice-cream

2 **Read the sentences, then listen and match the numbers to the letters.**

carrots

1 The new family restaurant

2 The food is

3 A meal for two

4 The service

5 *Laura's* is open

a costs about £25.

b from eleven in the morning till eleven in the evening.

c is on Bridge Street.

d very well cooked.

e is excellent.

potatoes

biscuits

apple pie

onion

garlic

bread

cheese

tomato soup

rice

grilled fish

pizza

sausage

crisps

steak

hamburger

chips

hot-dog

egg

bacon

pasta

tomato sauce

roast chicken

Reading

3 Read the text and: a) find any foods included in the pictures on p. 54; b) answer the questions below; c) explain the words in bold.

1 What is the name of the new restaurant?
2 What dishes can you have there?
3 What can you have for dessert?
4 What time does the restaurant open and close?

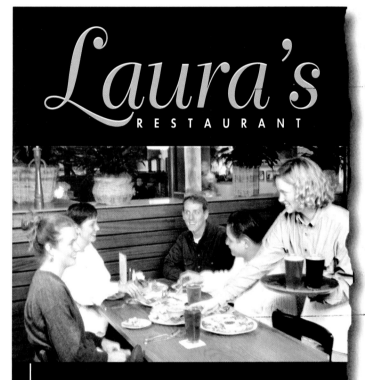

Laura's is the new **family restaurant** on Bridge Street and it's open for lunch and dinner every day.

The food is very well cooked. There are a lot of tasty dishes to choose from, such as pepper steak, roast chicken, fish with rice, tomato soup, pasta with rich tomato sauce, and lots of different salads. **Don't miss the chance** to try Laura's **home-made** bread — it's delicious! For **dessert**, have a **slice** of the chef's superb apple pie, or a **bowl** of Laura's special ice-cream.

A meal for two people costs about £25. The service is excellent, with very helpful and **friendly** waiters. The restaurant is open from eleven in the morning till eleven in the evening.

Laura's is a great restaurant for any **occasion**, but it is very **busy**, so **don't forget** to book a table first. (Tel.: 6640306) Enjoy your meal!

• Speaking

Read the text again and complete the table, then talk about *Laura's.* Start like this:

Laura's is a new family restaurant on Bridge Street ...

Name/Type:	*Laura's/family restaurant*
Location:	
Main Course/Dishes:	
Desserts:	
Cost:	
Service:	
Opening hours:	
Recommendation:	

Language Development

• Vocabulary

4 Choose words from the list to fill in the gaps, then use them to make sentences.

roast, apple, don't miss, helpful, home-made, tasty, book, tomato, pepper, special

1	.... steak	6	.... chicken
2	.... sauce	7	.... bread
3	.... pie	8	.... dishes
4	.... ice-cream	9	to .... a table
5	.... waiters	10	.... the chance

5 Complete the sentences with words from the list.

knife, fork, plate, frying-pan, spoon

1 We eat soup with a ....

2 We serve food on a ....

3 We cut food with a ....

4 We pick up food with a ....

5 We fry eggs in a ....

• Grammar: Plurals

6 Study the table, then complete the spelling rules.

SINGULAR	PLURAL	
loaf	- loa**ves**	Some nouns ending in -f or -fe drop the -f and take .... to form their plural.
cherry	- cherr**ies**	Nouns ending in a consonant + y, drop the -y and take ....
boy	- boy**s**	Nouns ending in a vowel + y take -s.
tomato	- tomato**es**	Some nouns ending in -o take ....

7 Write the plural forms of the words below.

1 potato 2 knife 3 strawberry 4 leaf 5 key

Countable - Uncountable Nouns

• **Countable nouns** are those which we can count. They have singular and plural forms. *1/2/3/4 apples*
• **Uncountable nouns** are those which we cannot count. They have only singular forms.
  some meat/sugar, etc
• **A/An** is only used with countable nouns in the singular. *a tomato/an egg* (NOT: *a sugar*)
• **Some** is used with either countable nouns in the plural or uncountable nouns. *some bread/some biscuits*

8 First, say which nouns are countable and which are uncountable, then fill in *a/an* or *some*.

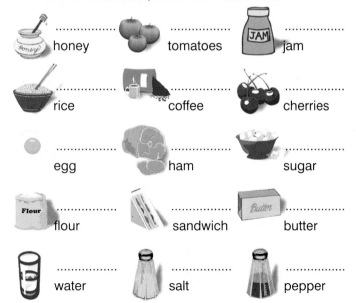

.... honey
.... tomatoes
.... jam
.... rice
.... coffee
.... cherries
.... egg
.... ham
.... sugar
.... flour
.... sandwich
.... butter
.... water
.... salt
.... pepper

We can use countable and uncountable nouns after phrases of quantity such as: **slice, bottle, glass, packet, kilo, loaf, cup, carton, piece** + of.

9 a) Fill in the correct words from the list.

slice, bottle, glass, packet, bowl, loaf, cup, carton, piece

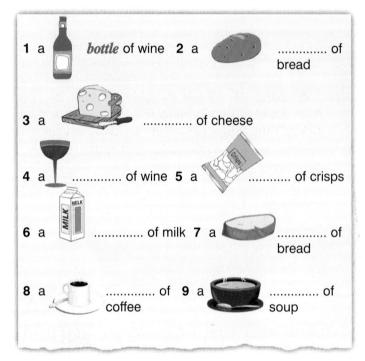

1 a *bottle* of wine   2 a .... of bread

3 a .... of cheese

4 a .... of wine   5 a .... of crisps

6 a .... of milk   7 a .... of bread

8 a .... of coffee   9 a .... of soup

b) Match these nouns to the words in the list in Ex. 9a.

Coke, flour, cake, juice, water, tea, cereal, sugar

10 📼 Listen to the dialogues and repeat. Then, use the prompts below to act out similar dialogues.

A: **I'm thirsty**. Is there anything to drink?
B: **Would you like** some orange juice?
A: No, thanks. I don't like orange juice.
B: **How about** some Coke?
A: Oh, yes, please! I'd love some Coke!

A: **I'm hungry**. Is there anything to eat?
B: **Would you like** a ham sandwich?
A: No, thanks. I don't like ham.
B: **How about** a cheese sandwich?
A: Oh, yes, please! I'd love a cheese sandwich!

• *coffee / tea*
• *beer / mineral water*
• *spaghetti / soup*
• *chips / hamburger*

• How Much/How Many - A Few/A Little

11 Study the examples and complete the rules, then use the prompts to act out similar dialogues.

SA: *How much* milk do you need?
SB: Just *a little.*
SA: *How many* carrots do you need?
SB: Just *a few.*

We use .... and .... with uncountable nouns.
We use .... and .... with countable nouns.

> ham, onions, flour, peppers, tomatoes, olives, bacon, cheese, bread, bananas, coconuts

12 *Julie is making a shopping list for a dinner party.* Look at the shopping list, then listen and tick (✓) the things she needs and cross out the things she doesn't need. Finally, ask and answer questions, as in the example.

S1: *How much* meat does she need?
S2: *She needs two kilos of meat.* How many eggs does she need?
S3: *She doesn't need any eggs. ...*

Shopping List

2 kilos of meat ✓
~~10 eggs~~
1 kilo of cheese
20 slices of ham
2 loaves of bread
1 kilo of tomatoes
2 packets of flour
3 bottles of Coke
1 carton of orange juice
8 bananas

• Some - Any

13 Study the dialogue below and: a) complete the rules; b) say which question expresses an offer and which expresses a request; c) use the prompts to act out similar dialogues.

SA: Is there *any* milk in the fridge?
SB: No, I'm afraid there isn't *any* milk. Would you like *some* Coke instead?
SA: Yes, please. I'd love *some.* Can I have *some* ice too?
SB: Yes, of course.

> We use **some** in the affirmative. We also use .... in the interrogative form for offers or requests. We use .... in the negative and interrogative form.

• orange juice - coffee - biscuits
• cheese - ham - bread
• bananas - strawberries - sugar

14 Listen to the dialogue and: a) fill in the missing words; b) say what the speaker says to accept the offer and what he says to refuse the offer; c) use the prompts to act out similar dialogues.

Would you like some coffee?

Yes, ... I'd love some.

Would you like some cake?

No, ... I don't like cakes.

• orange juice, chocolate   • wine, chips
• milk, biscuits   • lemon juice, cherries

15 Correct the mistakes.

1 I'd like ~~some~~ banana please.   ......a....
2 I'm thirsty. I'd like a water.   ....
3 Can I have any bread, please?   ....
4 I'm hungry. I like a hamburger.   ....
5 Would you like some tea? Yes, I love some. ....
6 Do you like a cup of tea? Yes, please.   ....
7 I'd like some sugars in my tea.   ....
8 How many honey do you need?   ....
9 Could I have a butter please?   ....
10 "Would you like some milk in your tea?"
   "Just a few, please."   ....
11 I'd like eggs but I don't like bacon.   ....
12 How many wine is there in the fridge?   ....
13 How much oranges do we need?   ....

• Reading & Listening

16 📼 **a) Read the sentences, then listen and mark them as T (true) or F (false).**

1 Brazilians don't like eating with their friends.   ....
2 Filipinos eat with a fork and a spoon.   ....
3 Finns like drinking wine.   ....

b) Read the texts and explain the words in bold. Then, read questions 1 to 8 and the texts again to answer the questions, as in the example. Finally, talk about people's eating habits in your country.

In which country/countries do they:

1 drink lots of coffee?   [A]
2 like sausages?   ☐
3 eat rice with every meal?   ☐
4 not eat in the street?   ☐
5 make very good beer?   ☐ ☐

6 usually eat dinner with their families?   ☐ ☐
7 sometimes eat with their hands?   ☐
8 never eat with their hands?   ☐

A BRAZIL

Whether at home **or** in a restaurant, Brazilians like eating with their friends and family. They never eat lunch at the **office** and they have dinner very late — at about ten o'clock at night.

Brazilians like small cups of **strong coffee**, at any time of the day. **As well as** many different fruit drinks, Brazilians also make very good beer. They don't eat in the street or on the bus, and they never eat with their hands. They always use a knife and fork to eat, even for pizza or sandwiches.

B THE PHILIPPINES

Many Filipinos have three meals a day with two **snacks** in between. Rice is a part of every meal — they even make desserts with rice and coconut milk. Filipinos like eating soup, meat, vegetables and a lot of different sauces. In some parts of the country, they make wine.

Families usually eat together and they like to **invite** people to eat with them. Filipinos eat with a fork and a spoon, or with their hands. It's **polite** to **leave** a little food on the plate at the end of a meal.

C FINLAND

There are a lot of different Finnish dishes, such as **smoked fish** and hot soups, but fast food such as pizza and sausages are also very **popular**. In the streets there are **stalls** which **sell** sausages, Finland's favourite food. Finns like drinking beer. They make excellent beer.

During the week, most families don't usually have dinner together. Sometimes at the weekends they eat with their friends. They cook meals together, or **each person** makes and **brings** a part of the meal.

Writing (Project)

Look at the Photo File section and complete the article about people's eating habits in Britain.

• Communication:
Ordering Food

17 📼 **Listen to the dialogue, then look at the menu and act out similar dialogues.**

Menu

Hamburger	£1.60
Fish and chips	£2.75
Cheese sandwich	£1.20
Drinks	
Coffee	85p
Tea	70p
Hot chocolate	95p
Coke (medium)	80p
Crisps	
Small packet	35p
Large packet	70p
Ice-cream	£1.80

SA: *Can I have a hamburger, please?*
SB: *Yes, here you are.*
SA: *Thanks. How much is it?*
SB: *It's one pound sixty. Anything else?*
SA: *No, thanks.*

British money:
£1 = one pound
£1.80 = one pound eighty
75p = seventy-five pence

1 pound

10 pence

18 Read the dialogue and fill in the missing words, then listen and check. Listen again and follow the text, then read out the dialogues.

W: Good evening, sir. Table for two?
M: Yes, please.
W: This way, please.
L: Thank you.
W: 1) .... you like to look at the menu?

• • • • •

W: May I take your order, please?
M: Yes. To start with I 2) .... the tomato soup.
L: Tomato soup for me, too, please.
W: Certainly. And for the main course?
M: I'd like the grilled fish.
L: And the roast chicken for me, please.
W: I'm sorry, madam. There's no more roast chicken tonight.
L: Oh. 3) .... I have a pepper steak, then?
W: Of course. 4) .... you like something to drink?
L: Just 5) .... water, please.
W: Very well. Would you like to order your dessert, now?
M: Yes. I 6) .... the apple pie.
L: Have you got 7) .... strawberries?
W: I'm sorry, we haven't. Would you like something else instead?
L: Just some ice-cream, please.

• • • • •

L: How is your fish?
M: Delicious. 8) .... about the steak?
L: A bit tough, but the sauce is nice.

• • • • •

W: Is everything all right?
L: Yes, thank you.
M: 9) .... we have the bill, please?
W: Of course, sir. One moment ...

• Vocabulary Revision Game

19 Work in teams. Take it in turns to choose words/phrases from the list and make sentences. Each correct sentence gets one point. The team with the most points is the winner.

how much, delicious, dessert, how many, helpful waiters, home-made, have dinner, lunch, cut food, choose from, I'd like, any, something else, tough steak

Pronunciation

20 Listen and tick. Listen again and repeat.

	/s/	/z/	/ɪz/
cakes			
loaves			
glasses			

	/s/	/z/	/ɪz/
sandwiches			
cherries			
carrots			

21 Listen and underline the correct items in bold in the table below. Then, use the notes to talk about the restaurant.

Name:	The Blue Lagoon
Type:	**Chinese / Hawaiian**
Location:	**Long/Short** Street
Main Course/Dishes:	fresh **fish/meat** dishes, Hawaiian burgers with pineapple
Desserts:	coconut **ice-cream/milk**, fried bananas in honey
Cost:	**£50/£30** for two people
Service:	excellent
Opening hours:	2 pm - **10 pm/12 am**
Recommendation:	very nice restaurant for the whole family, book a table

Writing (an advertisement for a restaurant)

Use the plan below and the information from Ex. 21 to complete the advertisement for *The Blue Lagoon* in the Photo File section.

Plan

Para 1: name of restaurant, type & location
↓
Para 2: dishes & desserts
↓
Para 3: cost, service and opening hours
↓
Para 4: recommendation

Words of Wisdom

Read these sentences. What do they mean?

• Man cannot live by bread alone.
• Eat to live, not live to eat.
• You can't make an omelette without breaking eggs.

● **Vocabulary**

1 **Underline the correct word or phrase.**

1 Mary is a(n) ***early bird/night owl***. She gets up at 5 o'clock every morning.
2 Snakes are ***mammals/reptiles*** and they lay eggs.
3 Ron's job is very ***tiring/boring*** because he works long hours.
4 Penguins have got thick ***fins/feathers*** to keep them warm.
5 We always wear heavy ***jackets/hats*** when we go skiing.
6 Cherries are my favourite ***fruit/vegetables***.
7 Use a ***spoon/fork*** to eat your soup.
8 John trains dolphins. He works at a(n) ***gym/aquarium***.
9 When it is hot and ***snowy/sunny***, we usually spend the day at the beach.
10 Sandy is really ***happy/bored*** with her new job. She likes it a lot.
11 Carol doesn't have any free time ***during/at*** the week.
12 Tigers are ***wild/farm*** animals. They belong to the cat family.

(12 marks)

2 **Use the words below to fill in the gaps.**

carton, loaf, long, chance, hours, decorate, books, home-made, rainy, funny

1 Doctors often work long ....
2 This restaurant serves .... apple pie.
3 It's a great film. Don't miss the .... to see it!
4 I would like a .... of milk, please.
5 We usually .... the Christmas tree a week before Christmas.
6 I like penguins a lot. They look very .... when they walk.
7 Could I have a .... of bread, please?
8 My father always .... a table at the Italian restaurant on Sundays.
9 I can't wear these trousers – they're too ....
10 The weather in Britain is often ....

(10 marks)

3 **Use the prepositions below to fill in the gaps.**

for, of, with, on, to, from, at, in

1 Steven and Jo aren't satisfied .... their new house.
2 My father never goes .... bed before 12 o'clock.
3 I love going .... long walks in spring.
4 Cows feed their babies .... milk.
5 My mother is afraid .... spiders.

6 Chimpanzees weigh .... 35 to 60 kilos.
7 Grandma is .... the kitchen .... the moment.

(7 marks)

4 **a) Use numbers to write the time.**

1 seven o'clock → ...7:00....
2 eight forty-five → ....
3 ten thirty → ....
4 a quarter past two → ....
5 eleven twenty → ....

(5 marks)

b) Look at the clocks below, and, in pairs, ask and answer questions, as in the example.

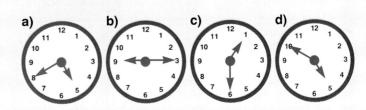

a) b) c) d)

SA: What time is it?
SB: It's twenty to five.

(4 marks)

● **Grammar**

5 **a) Use the verbs in the list to fill in the gaps.**

eat, are, live, weigh, have got, have, live for, swim

Blue whales **(1)** .... huge mammals. They **(2)** .... babies and feed them on milk. They **(3)** .... in oceans all around the world and they **(4)** .... plankton – tiny animals and plants that live in the sea. Blue whales can **(5)** .... very fast. They **(6)** .... up to 150,000 kilos! They **(7)** .... a very big tail and small fins. Blue whales **(8)** .... about 80 years.

(8 marks)

b) Put the words in the correct order to form questions, as in the example.

1 is/animal/this/what?
What is this animal?

2 they/live/where/do?
....

3 do/they/what/eat?
....

4 can/what/they/do?
....

5 they/how much/weigh/do? .
....

6 small fins/have/got/they?
....

7 live/they/do/how long?
....

(7 marks)

6 Underline the correct word or phrase.

1 *How much*/*How many* eggs do we need for the cake?
2 My sister *is playing*/*plays* in the garden at the moment.
3 Fish *can't*/*doesn't* sing and birds *isn't*/*can't* swim.
4 Grandpa *watch*/*watches* TV every evening.
5 Would you like *some*/*a* water?
6 They *never*/*ever* go to the beach on Mondays.
7 Have *sheep*/*sheeps* got wings? No, they haven't.
8 There is *any*/*some* milk in the fridge.
9 Susan often goes for long walks *in*/*at* spring.
10 Listen! The phone *is ringing*/*rings*.
11 Are there *much*/*any* strawberries in the box?
12 Could I have a *packet*/*carton* of crisps, please?

(12 marks)

● Communication

7 Use the words and phrases in the lists below to complete the dialogues.

please, here, can, would

a) A: **(1)** .... I help you, madam?
B: Yes, **(2)** .... I'm looking for a summer dress.
A: What colour **(3)** .... you like?
B: Blue.
A: **(4)** .... you are.
B: Can I try it on?
A: Yes, of course.

Would you like a, I'm hungry, How about some

b) A: **(1)** .... Is there anything to eat?
B: **(2)** .... piece of chocolate cake?
A: No, thanks. I don't like chocolate cake.
B: **(3)** .... apple pie?
A: Oh, yes, please! I'd love a piece of apple pie.

(7 marks)

● Reading

8 Read the text below and answer the questions.

Sarah Miles, 25, is a cook. "I like my job a lot because I love cooking. It is tiring, though, as I work from ten o'clock until eight every day," she says.

Sarah is not an early bird. Her day starts at nine o'clock. She gets up, has a shower and then drives to work. She arrives at the restaurant at ten o'clock, then she starts making the salads and desserts. At half past eleven, she has a break for lunch, then from twelve o'clock until five, she cooks for the customers. After that, she cleans the kitchen. She finishes work at eight o'clock, then she meets her friends. They usually go to the cinema or a Chinese restaurant in the evening.

In her free time, Sarah visits her parents or goes fishing with her brother. She also loves swimming. "I've got a great job and I feel very happy with the way I live," says Sarah.

1 Does Sarah like her job? Why (not)?
2 Why is her job tiring?
3 What does Sarah do in the morning/afternoon/evening?
4 What does Sarah do in her free time?
5 How does she feel about her life? *(10 marks)*

Writing

9 Use the information in the plan below to write an article about Fred King's daily routine and his free-time activities.

Plan

Para 1: Fred King, 38, reporter
"I like my job very much because I love interviewing people. It is tiring, though, because I work long hours."

Para 2: ● get up at 7 o'clock
● have a shower/get dressed
● leave home at 8 o'clock/arrive at the office at 8:30
● read the morning newspapers
● have lunch at 12:30
● in the afternoon/write articles/prepare for his TV programme
● TV programme/finish at 6 o'clock/then meet friends/have dinner
● in the evening/usually/watch TV or listen to music

Para 3: ● love sailing/not like playing football or basketball/go sailing every weekend

Para 4: ● "I have got a great job and I feel very satisfied with my life."

(18 marks)

TOTAL: *100 marks*

Moments in Life

◀ Read, listen, talk and write about...

Times Change...

Unit 9

• places & buildings

The Price of Fame!

• famous people & their achievements

Unit 10

Module 3

Units 9-12

All's Well That Ends Well!

Unit 11

Learn how to ...
- give directions
- ask for information
- ask personal questions
- report emergencies
- make comments
- make suggestions

Practise ...
- was/were – had – could
- past simple (regular – irregular verbs)
- prepositions of place/movement
- adjectives/adverbs
- comparisons
- quite/too/very/much

- feelings & reactions
- emergencies

See New Places, Meet New Faces!

Unit 12

- towns & cities
- means of transport

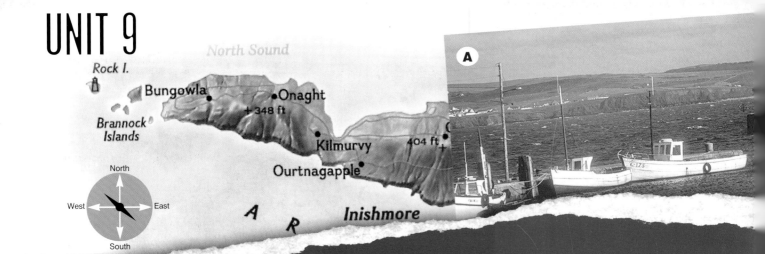

North Sound

Rock I.

Bungowla • Onaght
+ 348 ft
Brannock
Islands
Kilmurvy 404 ft +

Ourtnagapple

North
West ← → East
South

A R Inishmore

Times Change...

Lead-in

1 **Look at the pictures. Which picture shows:**

- fishing boats ☑
- a restaurant ☐
- a stone cottage ☐
- a ferry boat ☐
- an airport ☐
- a donkey ☐
- a bicycle ☐
- a souvenir shop ☐
- a guest house ☐
- green fields ☐

2 *Inishmore is a small island off the west coast of Ireland.* **Look at the pictures again and try to guess what there was/wasn't on Inishmore fifty years ago.**

3 📼 **Read the summary about Inishmore, then listen and cross out the wrong word.**

Fifty years ago, few tourists could reach Inishmore because there wasn't a(n) **1)** *port/airport*. Life was **2)** *difficult/easy*. Inishmore was a **3)** *noisy/quiet* place back then. Today there are cars, buses and ferry boats. The people have got new, modern **4)** *houses/cottages*. Inishmore is very **5)** *boring/busy* now. There are guest houses, restaurants and lots of **6)** *clothes/souvenir* shops. It is still beautiful, though.

Reading

4 Read the magazine article and answer the questions below. Then, explain the words in bold.

This week on our *Now & Then* page, we are looking at Inishmore, a beautiful little island off the **west coast** of Ireland. At first, Inishmore **seems** exactly the same as it was fifty years ago, but **in fact** it is a very different place today.

Colman Coneely, a 70-year-old **islander,** says, "When I was young, few tourists could **reach** Inishmore. There wasn't an airport or any ferry boats in those days. There were only donkeys and small fishing boats for **getting around**. Life was difficult. We didn't have much money — we only had small stone cottages. We didn't even have electricity or **running water**! Inishmore was a quiet place — there weren't any guest houses or restaurants back then."

Today, up to 2,000 tourists a day can visit Inishmore. "Now there is an airport," says Coneely. "There are also cars, buses, bicycles and big ferry boats. Life is very easy now. We have got new, modern houses and a lot of money. We have also got electricity and running water. Inishmore is very busy now. There are guest houses, restaurants and lots of souvenir shops."

Coneely looks across the green fields **in front of** his house and smiles. "Yes, Inishmore is beautiful and we're working hard to keep it just like this."

1 Where is Inishmore?
2 Could many tourists reach the island fifty years ago? Why (not)?
3 What did the islanders have for getting around?
4 What can you find on Inishmore today that wasn't there fifty years ago?
5 What does Colman Coneely think of the island?

● Speaking

Read the text again and make notes under these headings:

THEN	NOW
what there was/wasn't & what the people had/didn't have	what there is & what the people have got

Now, look at your notes and talk about what Inishmore was like fifty years ago and what it is like now. Start like this: *There wasn't an airport on Inishmore then. There were only donkeys and fishing boats ...*

Language Development

• Vocabulary

5 Choose words from the list to fill in the gaps, then use them to make sentences.

same, water, fields, cottages, houses, little, fifty years, shops, boats, like

1	a .... island	6	running ....
2	.... ago	7	just .... this
3	the .... as	8	modern ....
4	fishing	9	souvenir ....
5	stone	10	green ....

6 Write the opposites of the phrases below, using the words in the list. Then, make sentences using the phrases.

busy, big, a lot of

1 a little island ≠ a .... island
2 few tourists ≠ .... tourists
3 a quiet place ≠ a .... place

Inishmore is a little island.

7 Fill in the missing prepositions from the list.

in front of, on, off, back, in, across, at

1 .... our *Now & Then* page; **2** we're looking .... Inishmore; **3** .... first; **4** .... fact; **5** .... those days; **6** .... his house; **7** .... then; **8** .... the west coast; **9** look .... the green fields

8 Match the following with the signs.

1 The fire escape is on your left.
2 Turn right.
3 The fire escape is on your right.
4 Turn left.

a [ ]
b [ ]

c [ ]
d [ ]

• Grammar: Prepositions of Place

9 a) Look at the diagram, then complete the sentences with prepositions from the list below.

in front of, opposite, next to, on, between

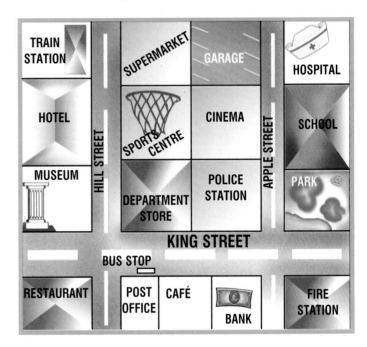

1 The school is .... the cinema.
2 The café is .... the bank and the post office.
3 The police station is .... the cinema.
4 The bus stop is .... the post office.
5 The park is .... the corner of Apple Street and King Street.

b) Where is: the sports centre? the hospital? the bank? the supermarket? the post office? the garage? the police station? the department store? the museum? the restaurant? the fire station? the school?

• Communication: Giving Directions

10 *You are at the train station.* Look at the town map in Ex. 9 and fill in the missing words. Listen and check your answers. Then, in pairs, use the prompts to act out similar dialogues.

A: Excuse me, **1)** .... you tell me the way to the bank?
B: Yes, of course. Go straight down Hill Street, then take the first turning **2)** .... Go down King Street. The bank is **3)** .... the café.
A: Thank you very much.

a You're at the bank and you want to go to the supermarket.

b You're at the supermarket and you want to go to the school.

c You're at the post office and you want to go to the sports centre.

d You're at the cinema and you want to go to the department store.

• Grammar: Was/Were (past simple of the verb "to be")

11 **Look at the table and complete the rules.**

Affirmative	Negative
I/he/she/it **was**	I/he/she/it **wasn't**
you/we/they **were**	you/we/they **weren't**
Interrogative	**Short answers**
Was I/he/she/it ...?	Yes, I/he/she/it **was**.
	No, I/he/she/it **wasn't**.
Were you/we/they ...?	Yes, you/we/they **were**.
	No, you/we/they **weren't**.

We use .... with I, he, she and it.
We use .... with we, you and they.

12 **Look at the list of prompts below, then, in pairs, ask and answer questions, as in the example.**

bicycles, fishing boats, restaurants, stone cottages, an airport, donkeys, souvenir shops, guest houses, green fields

SA: Were there any bicycles on Inishmore 50 years ago?
SB: No, there weren't. Were there any ...

• Communication: Asking for Information

13 📢 **Fill in** *were, was* **or** *wasn't,* **then listen and check. In pairs, use the prompts to act out a similar dialogue.**

at a restaurant - Sharon - the food - not very nice - horrible - Craig - at a football match

A: **1)** .... you at home last night?
B: No, I **2)** .... I **3)** .... **at the cinema**.
A: Who **4)** .... you with?
B: I **5)** .... with **Claire**.
A: How **6)** .... **the film**?
B: Well, it **7)** .... **very good**. It **8)** .... **boring**. Where **9)** .... you?
A: I **10)** .... at home.
B: **11)** .... you with **Sally**?
A: No, I **12)** .... She **13)** .... **at work**.

• Grammar: Had (past simple of "have")

Affirmative	I/you/he, etc **had**
Negative	I/you/he, etc **didn't have**
Interrogative	**Did** I/you/he, etc **have**?
Short answers	Yes, I/you/he, etc **did**.
	No, I/you/he, etc **didn't**.

14 **a) Look at the pictures. Tick (✓) what people had 100 years ago and put a cross (✗) next to what they didn't have. Then, in pairs, ask and answer questions, as in the example.**

SA: Did they have helicopters?
SB: No, they didn't. Did they have ...

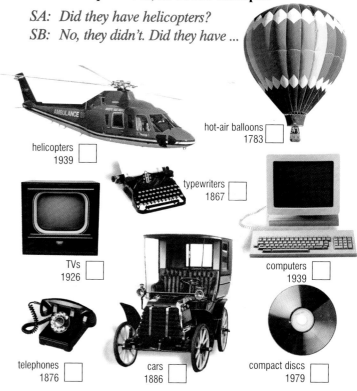

helicopters 1939 ☐
hot-air balloons 1783 ☐
typewriters 1867 ☐
TVs 1926 ☐
computers 1939 ☐
telephones 1876 ☐
cars 1886 ☐
compact discs 1979 ☐

b) Now write sentences, as in the example.

*They had hot-air balloons 100 years ago, **but** they didn't have helicopters.*

Writing (Project)

First answer these questions, then write a short paragraph (40-60 words) about yourself when you were seven years old.

a What was your best friend like?
b What was your favourite teacher like?
c What was your favourite toy?
d Did you have a pet? (What?)
e What was your favourite food/drink?

• Grammar: Could (past simple of "can")

Affirmative	I/you/he, etc **could** swim.
Negative	I/you/he, etc **couldn't** swim.
Interrogative	**Could** I/you/he, etc swim?
Short answers	Yes, I/you/he, etc **could.**
	No, I/you/he, etc **couldn't.**

15 📼 **a) Listen to the two men talking about themselves and fill in the missing ages in the table below. Then make sentences, as in the example.**
Paul **could** *talk* **when** *he was one,* **but** *Doug* **couldn't** *talk* **until** *he was two.*

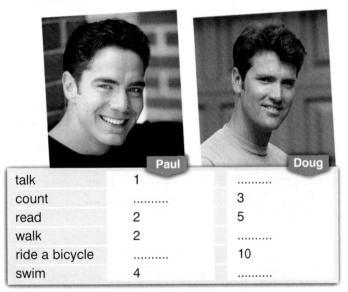

	Paul	Doug
talk	1	....
count	....	3
read	2	5
walk	2	....
ride a bicycle	....	10
swim	4	....

b) Now talk about yourself, as in the example.
I **could** *talk* **when** *I was one,* **but** *I* **couldn't** *count* **until** *I was three. ...*

• Reading & Listening

16 📼 **a) Read the sentences and explain the words in bold, then listen and underline the correct words.**

1 Some ancient Romans had beautiful **brick/stone** houses.
2 Ancient Rome had **wide/narrow** streets.
3 The public **baths/showers** were very popular.
4 Girls had **balls/dolls** to play with.

b) Read the text and fill in *were(n't), had, was* **or** *could(n't).*

Some ancient Romans **1)** .... very rich and they **2)** .... beautiful brick houses. There **3)** .... any windows on the outside walls and there **4)** .... any carpets on the floors. Other people **5)** .... smaller houses or flats. Ancient Rome **6)** .... narrow streets, but there **7)** .... lots of theatres. The public baths **8)** .... very popular. Men and women **9)** .... go there at different times, but children **10)** .... use the baths. Hunting, riding, fishing and having dinner parties with friends **11)** .... also popular free-time activities. There **12)** .... lots of games and toys for children. The boys' favourite games **13)** .... ball games and the girls **14)** .... dolls to play with. Children also **15)** .... dogs, cats, ducks and geese as pets. The ancient Romans **16)** .... lots of delicious food to eat, such as meat, fish, fruit, vegetables and bread, and their favourite drink **17)** .... wine.

c) Read the text again, then read the sentences below and circle the correct items.

1 The ancient Romans didn't have any .... in their houses.
   A tables   **B** carpets   **C** sofas
2 They had lots of ....
   A discos   **B** cinemas   **C** theatres
3 .... couldn't use the public baths.
   A Children   **B** Women   **C** Men
4 There were lots of .... and toys for children.
   A shops   **B** games   **C** schools
5 .... was one of their favourite free-time activities.
   A Dancing   **B** Playing football   **C** Hunting
6 Their favourite drink was ....
   A water   **B** wine   **C** milk

d) Talk about what the ancient Romans *could* **or** *couldn't do/* **what they** *had* **and what there** *was/wasn't* **in ancient Rome.**

17 Fill in the gaps with words from the list below.

can, can't, could, couldn't, was, wasn't, were, weren't, is, are, isn't, aren't, have got, haven't got, has got, hasn't got, had, or didn't have

1 A: ...*Can*... you swim?
B: No, I .... you swim when you .... five?
A: No, I ....

2 I .... a car now, but I .... a bicycle. I .... a bicycle when I .... six.

3 There .... a bank opposite the cinema, but fifty years ago there .... a bank — there .... a hotel, but it .... there now. There .... any shops then, but there .... a lot of green fields. Now there .... any green fields, but there .... a lot of shops.

4 When he .... five, he .... a cat as a pet. He .... any dogs. Now he .... three dogs, but he .... any cats.

5 When I was five, I .... ride a bicycle, but I .... ride a motor bike. Now I .... a motor bike and I .... ride it very well.

• Vocabulary Revision Game

18 Work in teams. Take it in turns to choose words/phrases from the list and make sentences. Each correct sentence gets one point. The team with the most points is the winner.

fishing boats, I didn't have, count, we could, reach, there weren't, green fields, pet, toy, there was, back then

Pronunciation

19 🔊 Listen and tick. Listen again and repeat.

	/ s /	/ ∫ /
shop		
sport		
shoe		

	/ s /	/ ∫ /
ship		
sun		
street		

20 🔊 *Ralph Cobbler is talking about Canary Wharf, an area in London.* Listen to what he says and complete the reporter's notes below. Finally, use the notes to talk about what Canary Wharf was like twenty years ago and what it is like today.

THEN	NOW
Canary Wharf was a **d**................ area twenty years ago.	Canary Wharf is a **c**................. area nowadays.
There were e.......... warehouses.	**There are b**.......................... flats, lots of shops, offices, restaurants and cafés.
There weren't m........................ shops or people.	
People didn't have m................. money or **n**.................... houses or cars.	**People have got** a lot of money, **l**.................. houses and **n**........... cars.
People could only get around by bus or on foot.	**People can** get around by train, bus or taxi.

Writing (a then-and-now article)

Use the plan below and the information from Ex. 20 to write an article (60 - 90 words) about Canary Wharf. Use the article in Ex. 4 as a model. Start like this: *This week on our Now and Then page, we are looking at Canary Wharf in London. This area is now completely different to what it was like twenty years ago.*
End like this: *Canary Wharf is a nice place to live nowadays.*

Plan

Introduction
Para 1: State the name of the place.
↓

Main Body
Para 2: Write what life was like **then** (what there was/were, there wasn't/weren't, what people didn't have and what they could do).

Para 3: Write about what life is like **now** (what there is/are, what people have got and what people can do).

Conclusion
Para 4: Say how nice the place is nowadays.

Words of Wisdom

Read these sentences. What do they mean?

- Times change and we with time.
- Other times, other manners.
- Time and tide wait for no man.

The Expedition

Sandra and David are in an aeroplane to Brazil. They want to write an article about the destruction of the Amazon rainforest.

ON THE PLANE ...

David, do you think the Jivaro Indians are dangerous?

I don't know. I hope not!

AT THE HOTEL ...

David, they called us from the reception desk. Our jeep is ready.

Let's go, then. Don't forget to take your hat. It's boiling hot out there.

IN THE JUNGLE ...

I don't like the jungle. It makes me nervous. I feel like someone is watching us all the time.

Don't be silly. It's so nice and peaceful here.

Sh!!! Listen! Can you hear the drums?

Oh no! It's the Jivaro Indians and they don't look friendly. Sandra, run! Let's go to the river.

Look ... a canoe! Quick! Let's get in it.

Come on! Paddle faster!

Calm down. They can't catch us now.

Sandra, watch your head!

Oh, no! A waterfall!

Help! Help! Help!

68

1 Look at the pictures on p. 68. Which picture(s) show(s):

a a jeep?
b a waterfall?
c a canoe?
d David and Sandra falling down the waterfall?
e David and Sandra on the plane?
f David and Sandra in a hotel room?

2 🔊 Who said the following? Listen to the story and write **S** (for Sandra) and **D** (for David).

1 It's boiling hot out there.   ....
2 I don't like the jungle.   ....
3 Someone is watching us.   ....
4 Let's go to the river.   ....
5 They can't catch us now.   ....
6 Oh, no! A waterfall!   ....

3 Read the episode and answer the questions.

1 What's the weather like in the jungle?
2 Why is Sandra nervous in picture 3?
3 Does David like the jungle? Why/Why not?
4 Who hears the Jivaro Indians first?
5 What do these phrases mean? "Watch your head!" "Come on!" "Calm down."

4 Match the adjectives to their opposites. Then, use the adjectives in the left column to make sentences, as in the example.

silly	safe
nervous	freezing cold
dangerous	noisy
nice	calm
peaceful	clever
boiling hot	horrible

Don't be silly.

a/an - the

We use **a/an** to talk about something for the first time. We use **the** to talk about something we have mentioned before. *There's a jeep outside. The jeep belongs to Mr Jones.*

We also use **the** before:
• the names of rivers (the Amazon River), seas (the Black Sea), oceans (the Atlantic) and mountain ranges (the Alps).
• nationalities (the English), the names of families (the Browns) and the names of tribes (the Jivaro Indians).

We don't use **the** before:
• proper names (Jane, Athens), the names of countries (Britain), the names of meals (breakfast) or the names of sports/games (tennis).

5 Read the summary and fill in *a, an* or *the*, where necessary.
.... David and .... Sandra go to .... Brazil to write .... article about .... Amazon rainforest. In the jungle, ... Sandra feels nervous. Suddenly, she hears .... Jivaro Indians. They run to .... Amazon River and get in .... canoe. David starts paddling down .... river in .... canoe. Suddenly, they see .... waterfall.

6 🔊 Listen to the episode and follow the dialogue. Then, take roles and read it aloud.

will

Affirmative	I/you/he, etc will go.
Negative	I/you/he, etc won't (will not) go.
Interrogative	Will I/you/he, etc go?
Short answers	Yes, I/you/he, etc will.
	No, I/you/he, etc won't.

We use **will** to make predictions. *I think the Jivaro Indians will catch them. Perhaps Sandra will hit her head.*

7 Match the objects to the words in the list, then make predictions, as in the example.

boiling hot, rainy, freezing cold, snowy

It will be boiling hot tomorrow, so don't forget to take your hat.

8 What do you think will/won't happen to David and Sandra? Use the prompts below to make one positive and one negative prediction.

they/die - they/break their legs - a crocodile/eat them - they/drown - they/hurt themselves - David/save Sandra - the Jivaro Indians catch/kill them - the Jivaro Indians/help them

The Jivaro Indians will catch and kill them. They won't help them.

The Price of Fame

Lead-in

1 Label the pictures with the names of the famous people.

Diana Spencer   *Leonardo da Vinci*
John F. Kennedy   *Marie Curie*
Elvis Presley   *Elizabeth I*
Rudolf Nureyev

2 Ask and answer questions about these people, as in the example.

S1: *Who was John F. Kennedy?*
S2: *He was an American president. When was he born?*
S3: *He was born in 1917. When did he die?*
S4: *He died in 1963.*

3 📼 Read the sentences, then listen and mark them **T** (true) or **F** (false). Who is this woman?

1 She had three older sisters.   ..F..
2 She worked as a nurse.   ....
3 The British loved her for her kindness and beauty.   ....
4 She died in a train accident.   ....

Reading

4 **a)** Explain the verbs in the list, then read Diana's biography and fill in the gaps with the correct verbs.

died, divorced, watched, studied, married, continued, returned, loved, said, worked, cared, completed, called, appeared

b) Explain the words in bold in the text.

A Queen of England (1533 - 1603)

B Polish scientist (1867 - 1934)

C Russian ballet dancer (1938 - 1993)

D American president (1917 - 1963)

E American singer and actor (1935 - 1977)

F Italian artist (1452 - 1519)

G Princess of Wales (1961 - 1997)

A Fairy-Tale Princess

*I*t was like a fairy tale when the beautiful young girl married the Prince and became the Princess of Wales. Unlike a fairy tale, the happiness soon ended, but Diana was still *The People's Princess*.

1 Diana Frances Spencer was born on 1st July, 1961, in Norfolk, England. Her father was Earl Spencer. She had two older sisters and a younger brother. Her parents **1)** .... when she was a young girl. As a child, Diana **2)** .... at a boarding school in Kent. She **3)** .... her **education** in Switzerland. When she **4)** .... to England she **5)** .... as a **nanny** in London.

2 Diana **6)** .... **Prince** Charles in July, 1981, at St Paul's Cathedral in London. People all around the world **7)** .... her **wedding** on television. Charles and Diana had two sons, William and Harry.

3 Diana was very popular. The British **8)** .... her for her **kindness** and beauty. They **9)** .... her "The People's **Princess**" because she **10)** .... so much about **sick** and **poor** people all over the world. She once **11)** ...., "I see myself as a princess for the world, not the Princess of Wales." Reporters were always around her. She was their favourite person.

4 But Diana's life wasn't as happy as it **12)** .... She and Charles had problems with their **marriage**. They finally divorced in August, 1996.

5 Diana **13)** .... to travel round the world and help those in need. But her life was short — she **14)** .... in a car accident on 31st August, 1997, in Paris. She was only thirty-six years old.

---

5 **Read the article again and match the headings to the paragraphs. Then, answer the questions below.**

- Everyone Loved Her ....*Paragraph 3*.....
- Diana's Early Years ....
- The Divorce ....
- The Tragic End ....
- The Wedding ....

1 When and where was Diana born?
2 Where did she study?
3 When and where did she marry Prince Charles?
4 How many children did they have?
5 Why was she popular?
6 Was her life as happy as it appeared?
7 When did they divorce?
8 When and where did she die?

● Speaking

Read the text again and complete the table. Then, talk about Diana, as in the example.
Diana Frances Spencer was born on 1st July, 1961, in Norfolk, England....

Name:	*Diana Frances Spencer*
Born on:	.... in ....
Studied at:	....
Married:	.... in .... at ....
Children:	....
Famous for:	....
Divorced in:	....
Died on:	.... in ....

Language Development

• Vocabulary

6 **Choose words from the list to fill in the gaps, then use them to make sentences.**

all over, worked, Princess, sick, car, in need, travel, fairy

1 she .... as a nanny
2 .... the world
3 .... tale
4 .... round the world
5 .... people
6 the .... of Wales
7 those ....
8 .... accident

Dates

We write: 26/8/1959 or 26th August, 1959
We say: the twenty-sixth of August, nineteen fifty-nine
          or
          August the twenty-sixth, nineteen fifty-nine

7 **Look at the dates and say them in the two ways shown above, as in the example.**

Elvis Presley

8th January, 1935
- 16th August, 1977

Alfred Hitchcock

13th August,1899
- 29th April, 1980

Johann Strauss

25th October, 1825
- 3rd June, 1899

Elvis Presley was born on the eighth of January, nineteen thirty-five and died ...
Elvis Presley was born on January the eighth, nineteen thirty-five and died ...

• Grammar: Past Simple

8 **Look at the table, then say how we form the past simple.**

Past Simple form	
Affirmative	I/you/he, etc watch**ed** TV last night.
Negative	I/you/he, etc **didn't** watch TV last night.
Interrogative	**Did** I/you/he, etc watch TV last night?
Short answers	Yes, I/you/he, etc **did.** No, I/you/he, etc **didn't.**

Use

We use the past simple for actions which happened in the past and won't happen again.
*Diana **married** Prince Charles in July, 1981. (When did she marry him? In July, 1981.)*
Time expressions: *yesterday, ago, in 1950, last Monday/week/month, etc.*

9 **Read the text, then ask your teacher the following questions to complete the text.**

Marie Sklodowska (Marie Curie) was a famous scientist. She was born in 1) .... in 2) ....
She studied physics and mathematics at the Sorbonne in Paris. She married Pièrre Curie in 3) .... Together they discovered 4) .... and .... in 1898. In 1903, the Curies received the Nobel Prize for Physics. Pièrre died in a road accident in 5) .... Marie continued their work on radium. In 1911, she received the Nobel Prize for Chemistry. She died of leukaemia in 6) ....

1 When was she born?
2 Where was she born?
3 When did she marry Pièrre Curie?
4 What did they discover?
5 When did Pièrre die?
6 When did she die?

10 **Write down two things you did yesterday and two things you didn't do yesterday. Choose from the list. You can use your own ideas.**

study, make a cake, play football, cut the grass, watch TV, cook dinner, listen to music, do the shopping, go for a walk, buy clothes

*I made a cake yesterday **but** I didn't cook dinner.*

11 **Fill in the missing prepositions from the list below.**

with, in, on, to, at, round, of

1 was born .... 1st July, 1961, ... Norfolk; 2 .... July, 1981; 3 studied .... a boarding school; 4 returned .... England; 5 .... St Paul's Cathedral, ... London; 6 watched her wedding .... television; 7 had problems .... their marriage; 8 travel .... the world; 9 those .... need; 10 died .... a car accident; 11 died .... leukaemia

Spelling

- We add **-ed** to most regular verbs.
  *I work - I work**ed***
- We add **-d** to verbs ending in -e.
  *I love - I love**d***
- Verbs ending in *consonant + y* drop the *-y* and add **-ied**. *I study - I stud**ied***
- Other verbs have irregular forms: *become - **became**, say - **said***. Look at the list of irregular verbs at the back of the book.

12 **Fill in the past simple forms of the verbs below.**

work	complete ....
watch	love ....
call	care ....
appear	divorce ....
end	continue ....
return	die ....

| study .... | **BUT** enjoy .... |
| marry .... | |

| write .... | make .... |
| buy .... | go .... |

13 **Put the verbs in brackets into the past simple. Which verbs are irregular?**

Sir Alexander Fleming **1)** .... **(be)** a famous scientist. He was born in Scotland on 6th August, 1881. He **2)** .... **(study)** medicine at St Mary's Hospital in London. After World War I, he **3)** .... **(return)** to St Mary's and **4)** .... **(work)** there as a professor.

In 1915, he **5)** .... **(marry)** Sarah Marion McElroy and they **6)** .... **(have)** a son. He **7)** .... **(discover)** penicillin in 1928 and **8)** .... **(receive)** the Nobel Prize for Medicine in 1945. His wife **9)** .... **(die)** in 1949. Fleming married again in 1953. His second wife **10)** .... **(be)** a Greek doctor, Dr Amalia Koutsouris.

Fleming **11)** .... **(die)** on 11th March, 1955. They **12)** .... **(bury)** him in St Paul's Cathedral.

14 **Match the paintings to the painters, then listen and check your answers. Now say who painted each painting.**

a. Pièrre-Auguste Renoir, b. Leonardo da Vinci, c. Edgar Degas, d. Frans Hals

1 ☐ Mona Lisa   2 ☐ Child with Cat   3 ☐ The Laughing Cavalier   4 ☐ Two Dancers

15 **Listen to these pieces of music. Number the composers in the order you hear their pieces of music.**

☐ Wolfgang Amadeus Mozart composed *Requiem*

☐ Johann Strauss composed *The Blue Danube*

☐ Antonio Vivaldi composed *The Four Seasons*

☐ François Chopin composed the *Polonaise - Fantaisie*

Writing (Project)

16 **First, put the verbs in brackets into the past simple. Then, match the sentences in column A to those in column B. Finally, write Mozart's biography.**

A

1 Wolfgang Amadeus Mozart was born in Salzburg, Austria, in 1756. He .... **(love)** music

2 He .... **(start)** writing music

3 He .... **(tour)** around western Europe with his father, Leopold

4 Everyone .... **(admire)** the talented young man

5 In 1781, he .... **(marry)** Constanze Weber, but life was difficult

6 Mozart .... **(continue)** writing music and performing at the royal courts of Europe

B

a) **and** they often .... **(invite)** him to their balls.

b) **and** .... **(learn)** to play the violin very well.

c) **when** he .... **(be)** five.

d) **because** he .... **(have)** money problems.

e) **until** he .... **(die)** in 1791. He was only 35 years old.

f) **and** .... **(play)** music for kings and queens.

• Reading & Listening

In the Public Eye ● ● ● ● ●

They are young, talented and famous.

They are the Backstreet Boys, or BSB

for short, an all-boy band from America.

Kevin   Nick

A.J.

Brian

Howie

The band started with Howie Dorough, AJ McLean and Nick Carter.

AJ worked as a model when he was six. He also acted in school plays. When he was fourteen, he got to know Howie. Howie had roles in films and plays. They became friends and went to auditions together. They met Nick at one of those auditions. Nick's parents had a disco and Nick used to dance there. The three of them started singing together for a record company called Transcontinental Records.

The record company owner, Lou Perlman, had a friend who knew Kevin Richardson. Kevin had a job at Disney World in Orlando at the time. When Lou's friend told Kevin about the new group, Kevin decided to meet them. The four became friends and Kevin joined the group. Lou wanted one more person for the group. The fifth member was Brian Littrell, Kevin's cousin.

BSB released their first album in 1996. They received their first gold record in Germany for this album. A second album followed in late 1997.

BSB have got fans in many countries. Do you want to write to them? Their address is: Backstreet Boys, Post Office Box 618203, Orlando, FL 32861-8203.

17 a) 📼 Read the questions, then listen and answer them.

1 Where are the Backstreet Boys from?
2 How many are there in the band?
3 When did they release their first album?

b) Read the text and explain the words in yellow, then underline all past simple forms.

• Speaking

c) Read the text again and correct the sentences, as in the example.

1 AJ worked as a model when he was three.
   Wrong! AJ didn't work as a model when he was three. He worked as a model when he was six.
2 AJ got to know Howie when he was thirteen.
3 Nick's parents had a theatre.
4 Kevin had a job at Disney World in France.
5 The fifth member was Kevin.
6 They received their first gold record in Italy.

d) Finally, in pairs, ask and answer questions about BSB using *who/where/when/what.*

18 Use the prompts and the time expressions below and, in pairs, act out short dialogues, as in the example.

WHEN was the last time you ...

write a letter?
visit your grandparents?
buy new clothes?
tidy your room?
wash the car?
have a haircut?
get a present?
have a party?

yesterday
yesterday morning/evening, etc
two days/weeks, etc ago
last Monday/Tuesday, etc
a week/month, etc ago

SA: *When was the last time you wrote a letter?*
SB: *The last time I wrote a letter was two days ago. How about you?*
SA: *The last time I wrote a letter was a month ago.*

• Communication: Asking personal questions

19 🔊 **Read the dialogue, then listen and fill in the missing words. Use the prompts to act out similar dialogues.**

A: **1)** .... was the last time you went shopping?
B: Last Monday.
A: **2)** .... did you go?
B: I went to Sainsbury's.
A: **3)** .... did you go with?
B: I went with my mum.

When was the last time you ...?
Where did you ...?
Who did you ... with?

go shopping
go to a park
go on holiday
go to a party
go on a picnic
go to a concert
go to the theatre
go out for dinner
go to the beach

• Vocabulary Revision Game

20 **Work in two teams. Take it in turns to choose words from the list and make sentences. Each correct sentence gets one point. The team with the most points is the winner.**

died in, scientist, fairy tale, died of, married, older sister, popular, poor people, divorced, marriage, studied medicine, discovered, buried, admire, invited, completed, composed, painted, discovered, received

Pronunciation

21 🔊 **Listen and tick. Listen again and repeat.**

	/ t /	/ d /	/ ɪd /
danced			
cooked			
played			
smiled			

	/ t /	/ d /	/ ɪd /
waited			
lived			
visited			
looked			

22 🔊 **Read the questions, then listen and circle the correct answer. Now, talk about Antonio Vivaldi's life.**

1 Who was Antonio Vivaldi?
A a painter **B** a composer and violinist
2 Where was he born?
A In Venice. **B** In Madrid.

3 When was he born?
A 4th July, 1678. **B** 4th March, 1678.
4 What did he become at the age of twenty-five?
A a priest **B** a teacher
5 Where did he teach music?
A at a school for girls in Venice
B at a school for boys in Venice
6 Did he travel to many countries?
A No, he didn't. **B** Yes, he did.
7 How many operas did he write?
A 40. **B** 30.
8 How many concertos for bassoon did he write?
A 30. **B** 39.
9 How many concertos for flute did he write?
A 39. **B** 30.
10 Was he a rich man at the height of his career?
A Yes, he was. **B** No, he wasn't.
11 Was he rich or poor when he died?
A He was rich. **B** He was poor.
12 When did he die?
A 28th March, 1741. **B** 28th July, 1741
13 Did he ever marry?
A Yes, he married twice. **B** No, he never married.

Writing (a biography)

When we write a biography about a person who has died, we **start** with the **person's full name**, what he/she is **famous for** and the **date** and **place** he/she **was born**. We then write about the **important events/achievements** in his/her **early** and **later years** in chronological order. We end the biography with **when** and **where** he/she **died**. We use past tenses.

Use the plan below and information from Ex. 22, to write a short biography of Antonio Vivaldi. Use Ex. 13 as a model.

Plan

Para 1: *full name, what he is famous for,*
↓ *date/place of birth*

Para 2: *important dates in his life in*
↓ *chronological order - early years/later years*

Para 3: *about his death*

Words of Wisdom

Read these sentences. What do they mean?

- The reward of fame and the price of fame.
- Actions speak louder than words.

UNIT 11

All's Well that Ends Well

Lead-in

1 **Look at the pictures, then read the questions and circle the correct answer.**

1 Where are the two people in picture A?
  a In a safari park.   **b** In an aquarium.
2 How do the lions look in picture A?
  a Friendly.   **b** Scary.
3 What is coming out of the engine in picture B?
  a Fire.   **b** Smoke.
4 What's wrong with the front of the car in picture C?
  a It's on fire.   **b** There's a lion on it.
5 What does a park ranger do?
  a He looks after a park.   **b** He puts out fires.
6 How do the people feel in picture C?
  a Happy.   **b** Scared.
7 How do they feel in picture F?
  a Shocked but happy.   **b** Tired and scared.

2 **Study the list of events below. Then, listen to the sounds and number the events in the order you hear them in the boxes provided.**

☐1 Claire laughed.
☐ They jumped out of the car quickly and ran to the jeep.
☐ The lions roared loudly.
☐ He tried to start the car several times.
☐ He stopped the car and started taking pictures of the lions.
☐ She beeped the horn and shouted for help.
☐ Just then, a park ranger came along the road in his jeep.

3 **Read the sentences, then listen to the story and write who said what. Write *C* for Claire, *G* for Greg or *P* for the park ranger.**

a "We don't want to be a lion's lunch."   ......
b "They're beautiful, but very scary animals."   ......
c "Let's go and see the gorillas, now."   ......
d "We'll burn alive!"   ......
e "Hold on, we'll get you out!"   ......

Reading

4 Read the story and answer the questions.

1 Where and when did the story take place?
2 What was the weather like?
3 Who are the two main characters in the story?
4 What happened to Claire and Greg?
5 Who saved them?
6 How did Claire and Greg feel at the end of the story?
7 What is the main event of the story?

One gorgeous, sunny day last summer, Claire and her friend Greg went to Longleat Safari Park.

When they drove into the park, they closed the car windows tightly. "We don't want to be a lion's lunch," Claire laughed. Soon, they saw some lions. Greg stopped the car very close to the lions and started taking pictures of them. The lions roared loudly. "They're beautiful, but very scary animals," Claire said. "You're right, Claire. Let's go and see the gorillas, now," Greg said. He tried to start the car several times, but nothing happened. Suddenly, smoke began to come out of the engine.

A few minutes later, the front of the car was on fire. They wanted to jump out of the car, but they couldn't because the lions were around it. They were both really scared. "We'll burn alive!" Claire screamed desperately. She beeped the horn and shouted for help. Just then, a park ranger came along the road in his jeep. "Hold on, we'll get you out!" he shouted. Almost immediately, another jeep arrived and chased away the lions. Claire and Greg jumped out of the car quickly and ran towards the jeep.

When they were safe inside the jeep, they thanked the park ranger for his help. They were still shocked, but happy. They knew they were very lucky to be alive.

Language Development

• Vocabulary

5 Write the past simple tense of these verbs.

1 go ....; **2** close ....; **3** come ....; **4** see ....; **5** stop ....; **6** chase ....; **7** start ....; **8** roar ....; **9** know ....; **10** try ....; **11** begin ....; **12** jump ....

6 Choose words from the list to fill in the gaps, then use them to make sentences.

beeped, burn, roared, tightly, park, lucky, chased, screamed, scary

1 closed the car windows ....
2 .... loudly
3 .... the horn
4 .... desperately
5 .... alive
6 .... ranger
7 .... animals
8 .... away the lions
9 .... to be alive

7 Fill in the correct prepositions from the list.
around, towards, on, in, into, out of, for, along

1 they drove .... the park; **2** the car was .... fire; **3** they jumped .... the car; **4** the lions were .... it; **5** she shouted .... help; **6** he came .... the road .... his jeep; **7** they ran .... the jeep; **8** they thanked him .... his help

We use **first, then, after that, just then, next, finally,** etc to talk about events which happened **one after the other**.
*Tony decided to go on a picnic. **First,** he made some sandwiches, **then** he packed the picnic basket. ...*

• Speaking

Read the summary of the story and underline the correct words in bold. Then, look at the pictures on p. 76 and give a summary of the story. Use *first, then, after that,* **etc where necessary.**

Greg and Claire decided to go to Longleat Safari Park. **1)** *First/ Next*, they drove into the park and Greg stopped the car. He took some pictures of the lions. **2)** *Finally/ After that,* he tried to start the car again. Suddenly, smoke began to come out of the engine. A few minutes later, the front of the car was on fire, so Claire beeped the horn and shouted for help. **3)** *When/Just then,* a park ranger came along in his jeep to help them. **4)** *Finally/ Last,* another jeep arrived and chased the lions away. Greg and Claire felt very lucky to be alive.

• Grammar: Prepositions of Movement

8 **Ralph went horse-riding in the countryside.** First, look at the pictures and use the prepositions to fill in the gaps in the text. Then, put the pictures in the correct order. Finally, look at the pictures and tell the story.

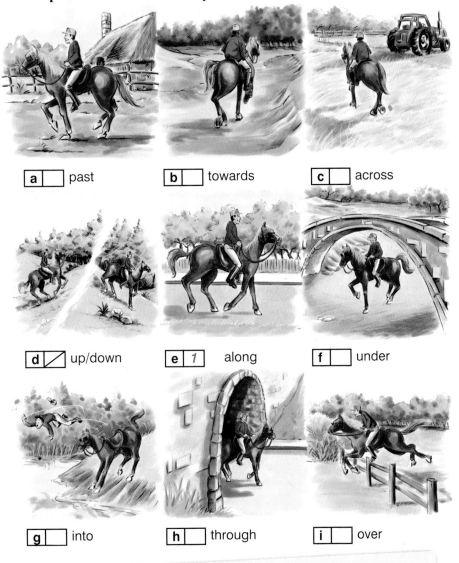

| a | | past | b | | towards | c | | across |

| d | / | up/down | e | 1 | along | f | | under |

| g | | into | h | | through | i | | over |

It was a lovely day, so Ralph decided to go for a ride in the countryside. He got on his horse and rode out of the field. At first, everything was fine. He went 1) ...**along**... the road, 2) .... the tunnel and 3) .... the forest. Then, he went 4) .... the hill. The view from there was beautiful! After that, he went 5) .... the other side of the hill, 6) .... a little old cottage and 7) .... the bridge. After that, he went 8) .... a field. Suddenly, everything went wrong! A tractor scared the horse and it jumped 9) .... the fence. Ralph fell off the horse and 10) .... the lake. He got very wet! It was a horrible experience!

• Grammar: Adjectives & Adverbs

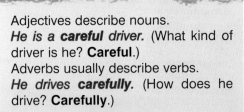

Adjectives describe nouns.
*He is a **careful** driver.* (What kind of driver is he? **Careful**.)
Adverbs usually describe verbs.
*He drives **carefully**.* (How does he drive? **Carefully**.)

9 The following adjectives and adverbs are from the story in Ex. 4. Underline them in the text and decide which are adjectives and which are adverbs. Which word does each describe?

1	gorgeous	..*adjective: day*..
2	sunny	....
3	tightly	....
4	loudly	....
5	beautiful	....
6	scary	....
7	desperately	....
8	quickly	....

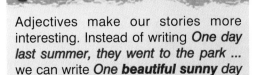

Adjectives make our stories more interesting. Instead of writing *One day last summer, they went to the park ...* we can write *One **beautiful sunny** day last summer, they went to the park ...*

10 Fill in the adjectives from the lists.

quiet, new, old, strange, white, bright, metal

a) Suzy got into her 1) .... car and started to drive home along a 2) .... country road. Suddenly, she saw a 3) .... light in the sky above her. She felt really frightened. Then, she heard 4) .... voices. She saw an 5) .... man with 6) .... hair and blue eyes. He had a 7) .... object in his hand and he pointed it at the car.

beautiful, sunny, shocking, white, happy

b) Everything was ready for Sally's wedding that **1)** .... day. She put on her **2)** .... silk dress and went downstairs. Just then, a **3)** .... bouquet of flowers arrived for her. Sally had a **4)** .... smile on her face. "From David," she thought. Suddenly, she screamed as she read the **5)** .... message on the bouquet.

11 **Study the examples, then complete the rules.**

Form & Spelling of Adverbs

- *He was a **careful** driver. He drove **carefully**.*
- *The **happy** child smiled. The child smiled **happily**.*
- *She was a **fast** runner. She could run very **fast**.*
- *They were **good** singers. They sang very **well**.*

- We usually form adverbs by adding .... to the adjective.
- When the adjective ends with a **consonant + y**, we drop the .... and add .... to form the adverb.
- Some adverbs have the same form as their .... hard → **hard**, fast → **fast**, early → **early** (**BUT:** good → **well**)

12 **Fill in the adverbs.**

ADJECTIVE	ADVERB	ADJECTIVE	ADVERB
hard	....	fast	....
strange	....	easy	....
happy	....	good	....
desperate	....	quick	....

• Grammar: Joining Sentences

We can join sentences with words such as ***and, but, because, so, then, when,*** etc.
Study the examples:
*She stood up **and** walked towards the door.*
*He looked out of the window, **but** he couldn't see anything.*
*He closed the window **because** it was very cold outside.*
*It was very late, **so** he decided to go home.*
*He opened the door, **then** turned on the lights.*
*He was in bed **when** he heard a strange noise.*

13 **Read the story in Ex. 4 again and find one example sentence for each of the following linking words:**
and, but, because

14 **Fill in** *and, but, because, so, then* **or** *when.*

1 The door was not locked, ... Mike opened it and went inside.
2 First, the sky turned grey, ... it began to rain.
3 We waited for Rob's answer, ... he said nothing.
4 Liz was in the kitchen .... the phone rang.
5 Mr Grant opened the letter .... read the message inside.
6 Mandy felt nervous .... the dog looked very scary.

When we start a story ...

we write **when** and **where** the event happened, **who** the people in the story were and **what** happened first.

15 **Look at the picture and read the short paragraph. Then, answer the questions.**

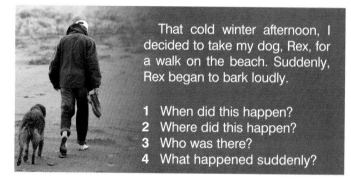

That cold winter afternoon, I decided to take my dog, Rex, for a walk on the beach. Suddenly, Rex began to bark loudly.

1 When did this happen?
2 Where did this happen?
3 Who was there?
4 What happened suddenly?

When we end a story ...

we write **what** happened in the end and **how** the people in the story **felt**.

16 **Read the story endings and underline the adjectives which show how each person feels. Which are positive? Which are negative?**

1 .... I felt very happy to be the winner of the competition.

2 .... Pam was really upset to see him leave.

3 .... He felt proud with the gold cup in his hands.

Writing (Project)

Look at the pictures in the Photo File section, then write a beginning and an ending for the story. Use the prompts.

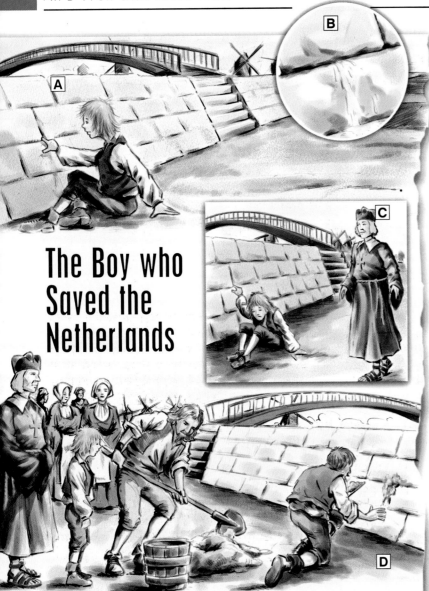

The Boy who Saved the Netherlands

• Reading & Listening

a) Look at the pictures. Which shows: a dike? a priest? a boy with his finger in a hole? people mending a hole?

b) Read the story and explain the words in bold. Then, underline the sentences which best describe each picture.
Picture A. - He put his finger in the hole, so no more water could come through it.

c) Read the events of the story below, then read the story again and put the events in the correct order. Finally, give a summary of the story using *first, then, after that,* etc, where necessary.

a		Hans heard the sound of water flowing away.
b		A priest heard Hans' cries and called some people to help.
c		The sky got dark and rain began to fall.
d	*1*	Hans Brinker went to visit an old blind man.
e		Hans put his finger in the hole.
f		Hans decided to return home.
g		The people mended the hole.
h		Hans noticed a very small hole in the dike.

d) 📼 Read the sentences, then listen and correct them.

1 Hans Brinker was ~~eighteen~~ years old. ..eight..
Hans Brinker wasn't eighteen years old. He was eight.
2 Hans visited a young woman. ....
3 Hans saw a big hole in the dike. ....
4 A woman heard Hans' cries. ....
5 A priest mended the hole. ....

e) Work in pairs. Use the prompts to ask and answer questions, as in the example.
Where/Hans/live?
SA: Where did Hans live?
SB: He lived in Haarlem, Holland.

1 How old / be / Hans?
2 Who / Hans / visit?
3 What / Hans / take / the man?
4 What / Hans / hear?
5 What / Hans / notice?
6 How long / Hans / stay / there?
7 Who / the priest / call?
8 What / the people / do?

Many years ago in Haarlem, Holland, there lived a young boy. His name was Hans Brinker and he was eight years old. One **autumn** day, Hans went across the canal to visit an old **blind** man. He took the man some biscuits and stayed there **for a while**. Then, Hans decided to return home.

"Be careful, Hans," said the old man. "The water in the canal usually gets higher in autumn." **On his way home,** Hans sang a song, watched the **rabbits** run around and picked some flowers for his mother. Suddenly, the sky got dark and heavy rain began to **fall**. Hans felt scared and started to run. Just then, he heard the sound of water **flowing** away. He looked around carefully, then **noticed** a very small hole in the dike.

Hans felt **frightened** because he knew what could happen. The small hole could **get bigger and bigger**. Then, the dike could **burst** and **flood** Holland! Hans knew what to do. He put his finger in the hole, so no more water could come through it. "Please, someone help me!" Hans shouted. But there was no one there to help him. After a while, he began to feel very cold and tired, but he could not leave the dike. All night long, Hans waited and waited ...

The next morning, a priest **walked by** and heard Hans' **cries**. "I'm trying to stop the water," the boy said. "Can you help me?" The priest called some other people and they quickly mended the hole. Finally, they took Hans home. Everyone was very proud of that **brave** little boy!

• Communication: Reporting Emergencies

18 🔊 **Listen to the dialogue. Then, in pairs, read the dialogue aloud. Finally, use the prompts below and your own name, address and telephone number to act out similar dialogues.**

O: Emergency services ... Which service do you require, please?
A: **Police**, please.
B: **Hill Street Police Station** ... Can I help you?
A: I want to report **a break-in** at my house. Please come quickly!
B: Could you give me your address and telephone number, please?
A: Yes — it's **5, Bond Road** and my telephone number is **9834758**.
B: And your name, please?
A: **Jack Ross**.
B: Thank you, **Mr Ross**. There's **a police car** on the way now.

• fire brigade
• Hill Street Fire Station
• a fire
• a fire engine

• ambulance
• Upton Hospital
• an accident
• an ambulance

• Vocabulary Revision Game

19 **Work in two teams. Take it in turns to choose words from the list and make sentences. Each correct sentence gets one point. The team with the most points is the winner.**

suddenly, roared, desperately, beeped the horn, scary, thanked, proud, mended, hold on, tightly, alive, shocked, for a while, on his way home

Pronunciation

20 🔊 **Listen and tick. Listen again and repeat.**

	/ʌ/	/ɒ/		/ʌ/	/ɒ/
wrong			shut		
rung			shot		

21 🔊 **Listen to the story, then try to fill in the gaps with adverbs from the list. Listen again and check your answers.**

desperately, immediately, suddenly, carefully, quickly, tightly, sleepily, nervously

a Tony .... heard noises.
b He went .... to the window.
c He ran .... downstairs.
d He .... rushed upstairs.
e He closed the door ....
f "Help!" he shouted ....
g He climbed .... onto a ladder.
h He climbed .... down.

Now, link the events using *first, next, after that, then* **and** *finally*.
Tony suddenly heard noises. First, he went sleepily to the window. Next, ...

Writing (a story)

When we write a story, we **start** by saying **when** and **where** the event happened, **who** the people in the story were and **what** happened first. We continue with **what** happened **just before** the main event **(2nd paragraph)**, then describe the **main event** of the story **(3rd paragraph)**. We **end** our story by writing **what** finally happened and **how** the people in the story felt. When we tell a story we use past tenses.

Use the pictures below and the events from Ex. 21 to write a story (100 - 150 words) for a magazine. End your story with ...
After all, he was very lucky to be alive!

Plan

Para 1: start the story (who the people in the story were, when/where/what happened)
↓
Para 2 - 3: develop the story (what happened before the main event/the main event itself)
↓
Para 4: end the story (what happened in the end - how he felt)

Words of Wisdom

Read these sentences. What do they mean?

• All's well that ends well. • A picture is worth a thousand words.

UNIT 12

See New Places,
Meet New Faces

Stratford-upon-Avon

Lead-in

1 *The pictures show views of Stratford-upon-Avon, a quiet town in England, and Los Angeles, a noisy city in the USA.* **Match the adjective-noun collocations to these places, then make sentences, as in the example.**
*Stratford is a **quiet** place, while LA is a **noisy** place.*
The streets in Stratford are ...

quiet	- noisy	place
clean	- dirty/polluted	streets
tall	- small	buildings/houses
cheap	- expensive	shops/hotels/restaurants
modern	- old	city/town
exciting	- boring	nightlife

2 **Look at the pictures and use the adjectives below to compare the two places, as in the examples.**

noisier, more expensive, cleaner, quieter, more modern, more polluted, cheaper, older, more crowded

*LA is **noisier than** Stratford.*
*LA is **more expensive than** Stratford.*

3 📼 **The sentences below describe LA. Try to fill in the missing adjectives, then listen and check.**

1 The hotels in LA are more **e**...................................... than those in many other American cities.
2 There are many **i**...................... places you can visit.
3 There are **f**..................... restaurants you can eat at.
4 You can buy **c**......................, fashionable clothes on Melrose Avenue.
5 The nightlife is **e**... .
6 LA is a modern, **n**......................... and crowded city.

Los Angeles

Los Angeles — The City of Angels

Los Angeles is <u>the</u> second <u>largest</u> city in America. It's also home to film stars, <u>sunny</u> weather, <u>tall</u> buildings and <u>heavy</u> traffic.

ACCOMMODATION

The hotels in LA are <u>more expensive</u> than those in many other American cities, but they are <u>clean</u> and <u>safe</u>. The Biltmore and The Omni are lovely, and close to special bus-stops where you can get <u>cheap</u> rides to the various sights.

PLACES TO VISIT

There are many <u>interesting</u> places you can visit, like Venice Beach with its street performers, Universal Studios to see how they make films, and Griffith Park. You can also see the handprints and footprints of film stars outside Grauman's Chinese Theatre. Children can visit the Children's Museum — one of <u>the most exciting</u> museums in the world.

EATING OUT

There are <u>famous</u> restaurants you can eat at, like the Buffalo Club, a place packed with celebrities, or Musso & Frank's, Hollywood's oldest restaurant. For <u>the most delicious</u> Mexican dishes, eat at the Border Grill.

SHOPPING

You can buy cheap <u>fashionable</u> clothes on Melrose Avenue. Do you want designer clothes? Then go to the expensive shops on Rodeo Drive. A visit there is always <u>unforgettable</u>.

ENTERTAINMENT

The nightlife is exciting on the Sunset Strip, an area in Hollywood with famous clubs like The Whiskey and The Roxy. There you can enjoy rock 'n' roll music. 24-hour cafés like Van Go's Ear are <u>popular</u> with visitors.

LA is a <u>modern</u> city with something for everyone. It's <u>noisy</u> and <u>crowded</u>, but it's also <u>fascinating</u>.

Reading

4

a) Look at the pictures on this page. Which shows: *heavy traffic; a museum; a street performer; handprints of film stars; a Mexican dish; designer clothes; a club?*

b) Read the article and answer the questions.

1 Where can you stay in LA? What is special about these places?

2 Which places can you visit? What can you see there?
3 Where can you eat? What is special about each place?
4 Where can you go shopping? What can you buy there?
5 Where can you go in the evening? What can you do there?

c) Replace the article's sub-headings with the ones in the list:
Nightlife - Restaurants - Shops - Hotels - Sights

• Speaking

Use your answers from Ex. 4 to talk about LA.

Language Development

• Vocabulary

5   **Choose words from the list to fill in the gaps, then use them to make sentences.**

film, heavy, 24-hour, sunny, designer, famous, expensive, make

1	.... weather	5	to .... films
2	.... traffic	6	.... clothes
3	.... shops	7	.... cafés
4	.... stars	8	.... restaurants

6   **Fill in:** *of, in, at, to, with, on*

1 the second largest city .... America; **2** it's home .... film stars; **3** close .... special bus-stops; **4** footprints .... film stars; **5** you can get rides .... the various sights; **6** eat .... a restaurant; **7** packed .... celebrities; **8** .... the world; **9** .... Rodeo Drive; **10** popular .... visitors

7   **Fill in the synonyms.**

district, not dangerous, memorable, well-known, interesting, near

1	safe -	4	famous - ....
2	close -	5	unforgettable - ....
3	fascinating -	6	area - ....

• Grammar: Making Comparisons

8   **Study the table, then say how we form the comparative and superlative forms of adjectives.**

	adjective	comparative	superlative
one-syllable adjectives	cheap large big	cheap**er** larg**er** big**ger**	the cheap**est** the larg**est** the big**gest**
-y adjectives	noisy	nois**ier**	the nois**iest**
adjectives with two or more syllables	expensive	**more** expensive	**the most** expensive
irregular adjectives	good bad much many little	**better** **worse** **more** **less**	**the best** **the worst** **the most** **the least**

The Colosseum
(82 AD)

The Great Pyramid of Cheops
(2465 BC)

The Parthenon
(438 BC)

Use

- We use the **comparative form** to compare **two** people, things, places etc. We usually use **than** with comparative adjectives.
  *The Parthenon is **older than** the Colosseum.*
- We use **the superlative form** to compare **more than two** people, things, places etc. We use **the ... of/in** with superlative adjectives.
  *The Great Pyramid of Cheops is **the oldest of** all.*
- We can also use **(not) as + adjective + as** to compare two places, things, people, etc.
  *Stratford-upon-Avon **isn't as noisy as** LA.*
- We use **much + comparative degree**.
  *Stratford is **much quieter** than LA.*

9   **Look at the underlined adjectives in the article about LA, then make a table and complete the missing forms, as in the example.**

adjective	comparative	superlative
large sunny	*larger* *sunnier*	the largest *the sunniest*

10   **Use the adjectives in the list to compare LA with the place you live in.**

large, clean, noisy, polluted, crowded, small, dirty, safe, expensive, old, modern, peaceful, cheap

*LA is **larger than** my town.*
*My town is **cleaner than** LA.*
*LA is **much noisier than** my town.*
*My town is **as noisy as** LA.*
*My town **isn't as polluted as** LA.*

11 📼 Read the sentences, then listen and put T (true) or F (false) next to each. Finally, agree or disagree with the statements, as in the examples.

London

Edinburgh

1 Edinburgh is smaller than London. *T*
That's true. London isn't as small as Edinburgh. ....
Actually, Edinburgh is much smaller than London.

2 Edinburgh is more dangerous than London. *F*
That's false. Edinburgh isn't as dangerous as London. Actually, London is much more dangerous than Edinburgh.

3 Edinburgh is noisier than London. ....

4 London is more polluted than Edinburgh. ....

5 London is cheaper than Edinburgh. ....

12 📼 Fill in the superlative forms and choose the correct item. Then, listen and check your answers.

1 Which is .... (large) desert in the world?
A the Sahara   **B** the Gobi   **C** the Nevada

2 Which is .... (high) mountain in the world?
A Ben Nevis   **B** Mount McKinley   **C** Mount Everest

3 Which is .... (long) river in the world?
A the Missouri   **B** the Mississippi   **C** the Nile

4 Where is .... (dry) place in the world?
A in Chile   **B** in Canada   **C** in China

5 Which is .... (small) country in the world?
A Luxembourg   **B** Wales   **C** the State of the Vatican City

6 Where is .... (hot) place in the world?
A Death Valley   **B** Tokyo   **C** Malta

7 Which is .... (tall) building in the USA?
A the Empire State Building   **C** the Sears Tower
B the John Hancock Centre

● Speaking

Ask and answer questions, as in the example.

S1: Which is the largest desert in the world?
S2: The largest desert in the world is the Sahara. Which ...

13 Look at the table, then make sentences, as in the examples.

	BUSES	TRAINS	TAXIS
expensive	✓	✓✓	✓✓✓
safe	✓✓	✓✓✓	✓
fast	✓	✓✓✓	✓✓
comfortable	✓	✓✓✓	✓✓

Buses in Britain are expensive.
*Trains in Britain are **more expensive than** buses.*
*Taxis in Britain are **the most expensive of** all.*
*Buses in Britain aren't **as expensive as** taxis.*

14 In pairs, talk about your city/town using the prompts below, as in the example.

old building, large park, busy road, popular café, expensive restaurant, famous square, pretty building

SA: Which is the oldest building in ...?
SB: I think the Town Hall is the oldest building in my city. Which is the largest park?

Writing (Project)

Which is the oldest building, the largest park, the busiest road, the most popular café, the most expensive restaurant, the most famous square/building in your town/city? Write a short paragraph about your town/city.
Start like this: *I live in ... . It is in ...*

● Communication: Making Comments

15 📼 First, listen and repeat. Then, take roles and act out the dialogues.

a David: What was New York like?
Julie: Great! The people were really friendly and there were lots of interesting places to visit!

b Mary: Did you like Ibiza?
Tony: No, I hated it. It was too crowded and the hotel was too noisy.

c John: What did you think of Paris?
Sarah: It was fantastic! It had some excellent shops and we ate at some wonderful restaurants.

• Communication: Making Suggestions

To make suggestions we use expressions like:
Let's ..., Shall we ...?, Why don't we ...?
Let's go to Rome this year./*Shall we* go to Rome this year?/*Why don't we* go to Rome this year?

16 a) **Study the examples and the key language, then read the dialogue and fill in** *quite, very, much* **or** *too.* **Listen and check your answers.**

> *quite* noisy (+), **very** noisy (++),
> **much** noisier (+++), **too** noisy (−)

John has got £100 and wants to spend a weekend at a hotel by the sea.

HOTEL A costs £30.	It's **very** cheap.	
HOTEL B costs £50.	It's **quite** cheap.	
HOTEL C costs £40.	It's **much** cheaper than hotel B.	
HOTEL D costs £70.	It's **quite** expensive.	
HOTEL E costs £95.	It's **very** expensive	
HOTEL F costs £120.	It's **too** expensive. (He's only got £100.)	

A: Shall we go to Mykonos for our summer holidays?
B: Well, it looks **1)** .... (++) **nice**, but I think it's **2)** .... (−) **expensive** for us.
A: Why don't we go to Santorini then? It's **3)** .... (+) **cheap** and **4)** .... (++) **pretty**.
B: Okay! Let's go there then. It's **5)** .... (+++) **cheaper** than Mykonos.

b) **Work in pairs. Use the prompts to act out similar dialogues.**

pretty (++), noisy (−)   quiet (+), beautiful (++)

beautiful (++), crowded (−)   sunny (+), exciting (++)

17 *Patsy and Bob are trying to choose a hotel to stay at during their holiday.* **Read the dialogue and fill in the comparative and superlative forms, then listen and check. In pairs, read out the dialogue.**

Bob: What are you doing, Patsy?
Patsy: I'm looking at the holiday brochure again. There are three hotels in the town, but I can't decide which one we should stay at.
Bob: Let me see. Hmm ... why don't we stay at the Sunset? It looks the **1)** .... (**comfortable**) of the three, and it's not as **2)** .... (**expensive**) as the Grand.
Patsy: That's true, but it's on the main road, next to all the discos and cafés.
Bob: So? That means it's in the **3)** .... (**convenient**) part of town.
Patsy: But I'm sure it's much **4)** .... (**noisy**) than the other hotels.
Bob: What about the Seaview, then?
Patsy: Well, it is the **5)** .... (**cheap**) hotel in town, and it's probably **6)** .... (**quiet**) than the Sunset.
Bob: Shall we stay at the Seaview, then?
Patsy: I don't know. It looks quite dirty, don't you think?
Bob: Perhaps it's not as **7)** .... (**clean**) as the others, but the brochure says it's got the "**8)** .... (**friendly**) staff in town."
Patsy: I like the Grand. It's the **9)** .... (**luxurious**) of the three hotels, and it's the **10)** .... (**close**) to the beach.
Bob: But it's too expensive! We can't afford it, Patsy!
Patsy: Oh, I suppose you're right. Okay, let's stay at the Seaview. I'm sure it will be fine ...

• Vocabulary Revision Game

18 **Work in two teams. Take it in turns to choose words from the list and make sentences. Each correct sentence gets one point. The team with the most points is the winner.**

clean, quieter, more polluted, oldest, interesting, street performers, designer clothes, nightlife, sunny weather, heavy traffic, fashionable clothes, delicious, noisier, more expensive, crowded

- Reading & Listening

19 **a)** 🎞 **The following statements are about Stratford-upon-Avon. Read them, then listen and underline the correct word.**

a It is **Shakespeare's / Duke's** birthplace.
b Have lunch at one of the many restaurants in **Sheep / High** Street.
c Stratford is a **big / small** town.

STRATFORD-UPON-AVON

This romantic town is in the south-west of England and is Shakespeare's birthplace.

A ....

The Dukes Hotel and The Swans Nest are two lovely places to stay in Stratford. The Dukes Hotel is a three-star hotel in the centre of the town, and The Swans Nest is next to the River Avon. They are both quiet and friendly places.

B ....

For sightseeing, get on an open-topped double-decker bus and see the town. You can also visit New Place — Shakespeare's home, or go for a walk in the beautiful Bancroft Gardens and see the open-air entertainers. Another fascinating place to visit is Warwick Castle, one of the oldest castles in Britain.

C ....

There are some fantastic restaurants in Stratford, too. Have lunch at one of the many restaurants in Sheep Street — the food is delicious — or have a romantic dinner at the restaurant on a canal boat in the Canal Basin.

D ....

Buy yourself something nice in one of Stratford High Street's excellent shops. However, for gifts, the street market in Rother Street is the best.

E ....

Stratford is a small town. There aren't many nightclubs, but you can spend an evening at the Royal Shakespeare Theatre or enjoy a quiet drink at one of the town's friendly pubs. You can also go for a walk along the riverside and enjoy the peacefulness of the place under the moon and stars.

Stratford is the ideal place for an interesting holiday. Don't miss the chance to visit it.

b) **Fill in the gaps in the text with the appropriate sub-headings.**
Eating out, Places to Visit, Nightlife, Shopping, Accommodation
c) **Read the text and take notes under the sub-headings.**
Now, look at your notes and talk about Stratford-upon-Avon.

Pronunciation

20 🎞 **Listen and tick. Listen again and repeat.**

	/tʃ/	/dʒ/		/tʃ/	/dʒ/
chin			chain		
gin			cherry		
Jane			Jerry		

Writing (a description of a place)

When we write an **article** for a **magazine describing a place**, we may give the information under suitable **sub-headings**.

We **start** by stating the **name** of the place and its **location**, then we give a **short** general **description** of the place.

After that, we talk about where visitors can **stay** (accommodation), **places** to **visit** or **eat** at, where to **go shopping** and the **nightlife.**

We **end** by giving an **overall impression** of the place. Adjectives make our description more interesting.

We normally use present tenses in this type of writing.

Look at the information in the Photo File section, then write an article about Antwerp. Give the information under suitable sub-headings (120 - 150 words).

Words of Wisdom

Read these sentences. What do they mean?

- See new places, meet new faces.
- Absence makes the heart grow fonder.
- Out of sight, out of mind.

1 Look at the pictures then read the sentences and circle the correct item.

1 *A snake/An alligator* is after David.
2 David and Sandra meet *a doctor/the Indians' chief*.
3 The Indian wants to see Sandra's *bag/camera*.
4 Mike is *satisfied/disappointed*.

2 📟 Who said the following? Listen to the episode and write **S** (for Sandra), **D** (for David), **H** (for Doctor Hamperdin) or **M** (for Mike).

1 Here, hold on to this. ....
2 Don't be afraid. ....
3 Everybody thinks that you're dead. ....
4 He won't hurt you. ....
5 The Jivaro Indians love their land. ....
6 Good work, you two. ....

3 Match the captions to the pictures.

1 the destruction of the rainforest
2 Some people kill the animals.
3 People cut down trees.
4 The Jivaro Indians use some plants as medicine.

A
B
C

D

4 Read the episode and answer the questions.

1 Who saved David from the alligator?
2 Who was the man Sandra and David met?
3 Who saved Doctor Hamperdin?
4 Where does he live now?
5 What is he doing in the rainforest?
6 What don't the Jivaro Indians want?
7 Does Doctor Hamperdin want to go back?
8 What does David need to buy? Why?

5 📟 Listen to the episode and follow the dialogue. Then take roles and read it out.

6 Fill in the past simple and underline the correct linking word.

David **1)** .... (be) scared **and/because** an alligator **2)** .... (be) after him. David and Sandra **3)** .... (be) on the river bank **when/so** they **4)** .... (see) the Jivaro Indians with a white man. Sandra **5)** .... (not/know) him **then/but** David **6)** .... (recognise) him as Doctor Hamperdin. David **7)** .... (be) confused **and/so** Doctor Hamperdin **8)** .... (explain) that he lived with the Jivaro Indians after his accident. He **9)** .... (say) the Indians **10)** .... (love) their land **and/but** they **11)** .... (want) to protect it. He **12)** .... (promise) to help them write their article **then/so** he **13)** .... (ask) them not to tell anyone about him.

7 Read the events and put them in the correct order, then tell the story.

☐ They found a canoe.
☐ Doctor Hamperdin told them about the Jivaro Indians.
☑ Sandra and David got on a plane to Brazil.
☐ They went to the jungle.
☐ They fell down a waterfall.
☐ They heard drums and saw the Jivaro Indians.
☐ They met Doctor Hamperdin.
☐ Mike was satisfied with their article.
☐ They ran to the river.
☐ Sandra saved David from an alligator.
☐ Sandra and David came back to London.

8 Read the text and fill in the missing adjectives from the list.

many, large, serious, longest, whole

The Amazon Rainforest is a **1)** .... beautiful forest in Brazil, South America. It lies at the mouth of the Amazon River. The Amazon river is the **2)** .... river in South America. It runs between the Andes Mountain Ranges and the Atlantic Ocean.

The Amazon Rainforest is a very beautiful place. A wide variety of animals, birds and insects live in it. There are also **3)** .... trees and plants.

Today, the forest has a very **4)** .... problem. People are cutting down too many of its trees. As a result, much of its animal and plant life is disappearing forever. Trees and plants are very important to the environment. Some scientists say that the **5)** .... world is in danger because of the destruction of the rainforests.

89

• Vocabulary

1 **Fill in the gaps with the words below.**

fans, guest, beeped, completed, get around, home, souvenir, heavy, roared, birthplace

1 There is a lot of .... traffic in the city centre.
2 The children were scared when the lions ....
3 Peter .... the horn and shouted for help.
4 Princess Diana .... her education in Switzerland.
5 They stayed in a wonderful .... house by the sea.
6 Tupelo, Mississippi is Elvis Presley's ....
7 You can only .... the island on foot.
8 Paris is .... to many famous actors.
9 The band has got .... in many countries.
10 We stopped at a .... shop to buy gifts.

(10 marks)

2 **Underline the correct adjective.**

1 The streets in LA are very **crowded/heavy**.
2 The street was too **narrow/wide**. Tom couldn't drive along it.
3 Big cities are often **quiet/noisy** and polluted.
4 He couldn't buy the shoes because they were too **expensive/cheap**.
5 He's a very **clever/silly** child. He knows all the answers.
6 Don't go near the river, it's very **safe/dangerous**.
7 That is a(n) **easy/difficult** question. I can't answer it.
8 It was a boiling **cold/hot** day, so we went to the beach.
9 He wasn't scared when the fire started. He was very **brave/blind**.
10 I like my teacher. His lessons are very **interesting/dull**.

(10 marks)

3 **Fill in the correct preposition from the list.**

on, with, at, in, to

1 The shop was packed .... fashionable clothes.
2 This is the most peaceful place .... the world.
3 My school is close .... my house.
4 Football is popular .... children.
5 To get to the station, take the second turning .... your left.
6 Bob wants to study .... Oxford University.
7 Alex was born .... 6th August, 1981.
8 John F. Kennedy died .... 1963.

(8 marks)

4 **Fill in the correct adverb.**

1 loud	-		5 happy	- ....
2 tight	-		6 careful	- ....
3 sleepy	-		7 desperate	- ....
4 nervous	-		8 good	- ....

(8 marks)

• Grammar

5 **Fill in the correct form of the verbs in brackets.**

1 When .... **(be)** the last time you .... **(tidy)** your room?
2 They .... **(go)** to Malta last month.
3 Yesterday we .... **(cut)** the grass , then we .... **(wash)** the car.
4 When we .... **(go)** to Europe last year we .... **(drive)** through France and Italy.
5 They .... **(not/play)** my favourite song at the concert yesterday.
6 The last time I .... **(have)** a haircut was two weeks ago.
7 My sister .... **(make)** a beautiful cake yesterday and I .... **(cook)** dinner.
8 Sally .... **(not/visit)** her grandparents last Christmas, so she .... **(write)** them a letter.
9 Yesterday we .... **(take)** the camera with us, but we .... **(not/take)** any pictures.

(9 marks)

6 **Fill in the gaps with words from the list.**

have got, wasn't, were, couldn't, was, weren't, is, are, can, could, haven't got

1 Today she .... a famous film star, but when she was twenty years old she ....
2 There .... six members in the band now. Three years ago there .... only four members.
3 A: .... you play the guitar well when you were twelve?
   B: No, I ...., but I .... play it well now.
4 I .... five brothers, but I .... any sisters.
5 When I .... young, there .... any nightclubs in the town.

(5 marks)

7 **Underline the correct word.**

1 A: Chris thinks Jenny is **most/more** beautiful than Mary.
  B: She is, but she isn't as **cleverer/clever** as Mary.
2 A: This is the **luxurious/most luxurious** hotel of all.
  B: But it's on the **noisier/noisiest** street in Rome.
3 A: Was Claire **scary/scared** when she saw the lions?
  B: Yes, and she screamed **desperately/desperate**.
4 A: Sam's motorbike is much **bigger/biggest** than Tom's or Frank's.
  B: It's also the **more/most** expensive of all.
5 A: This dress is prettier **as/than** that one.
  B: Yes, and it is also the cheapest **of/in** all.
6 A: The black shoes are **cheaper/cheapest** than the blue shoes.
  B: Are they **as/much** comfortable as the blue ones?
7 A: Did the footballers play **good/well** yesterday?
  B: No, they didn't. They played very **badly/bad**.

(7 marks)

8 **Match the numbers to the letters to make sentences.**

1 The children couldn't go to the concert
2 Paul married Elizabeth
3 We were in the fishing boat
4 I wanted to make a cake,
5 First, they got into the canoe,
6 Roberta didn't like any of the souvenirs,

a but I didn't have any sugar or flour.
b because they didn't have any money.
c so she didn't buy any.
d and they had four children.
e then they started paddling down the river.
f when it started to rain.

(6 marks)

• **Communication**

9 **Fill in the gaps with phrases from the list.**

lucky to be alive, I suppose, back then, though, who did, was fantastic, did you go, can you tell me

1 A: Grandad, what was it like when you were a boy?
  B: Oh, life was very difficult **1)** ....!

2 A: We can't afford this hotel. It's too expensive!
  B: Oh, **2)** .... you're right. Let's look for something cheaper.

3 A: Lions are very dangerous animals. You're **3)** ....!
  B: Yes, I know. I was nearly a lion's lunch!

4 A: My house is very old.
  B: Yes, it is. It's very beautiful, **4)** ....

5 A: Where **5)** .... last weekend?
  B: I went to the art museum.

6 A: Excuse me, **6)** .... the way to the post office?
  B: Yes, of course. Go down this street and turn left.

7 A: **7)** .... Mother go shopping with?
  B: She went with Aunt May.

8 A: Did you enjoy your holiday?
  B: Yes, it **8)** ....!

(8 marks)

• **Reading**

10 **Fill in the correct words from the list, then ask and answer questions about Winston Churchill.**

education, famous, born, helped, studied, loved, worked, married, died

Winston Churchill was a **1)** .... British politician. He was **2)** .... in Oxfordshire, England, on 30th November, 1874.

He **3)** .... at the Royal Military College in Sandhurst. After he completed his **4)** .... in 1896, he became a journalist and **5)** .... for a newspaper. Three years later he became a politician.

He became Prime Minister in 1940. He was very popular. The people **6)** .... him for his strength and wisdom. He **7)** .... his country very much during the Second World War. He **8)** .... Clementine Hozier in 1908.

Churchill **9)** .... at home in 1965. He was 91 years old.

(9 marks)

Writing

11 **Study the information below, then write a short biography of Bette Davis.**

BETTE DAVIS

famous film and theatre actress

BORN: Lowell, Massachusetts, in the USA / 5th April, 1908
STUDIED: drama / New York
1931: go to Hollywood
1935: win / Oscar for Best Actress
POPULAR: because of her beauty and talent
MARRIED: Gary Marrill / 1950
DIED: 1989 / Paris, France

(20 marks)

TOTAL: *100 marks*

What the Future Holds ....

◀ **Read, listen, talk and write about...**

Time Will Tell!

- future plans/intentions/predictions
- horoscopes

Unit 13

Dos and Don'ts

Unit 14

- the environment
- tips & rules

Module 4

Units 13-15

◀ **Learn how to ...**
- accept/refuse invitations
- give advice
- give/refuse permission
- express obligation/prohibition
- make a reservation
- invite someone out
- buy souvenirs

◀ **Practise ...**
- be going to/will/Present continuous (future meaning)
- there/it will be
- modals (should, shouldn't, must, mustn't, can, can't)
- present perfect

Take a Break!

Unit 15

- holidays & sights

UNIT 13

Time will Tell

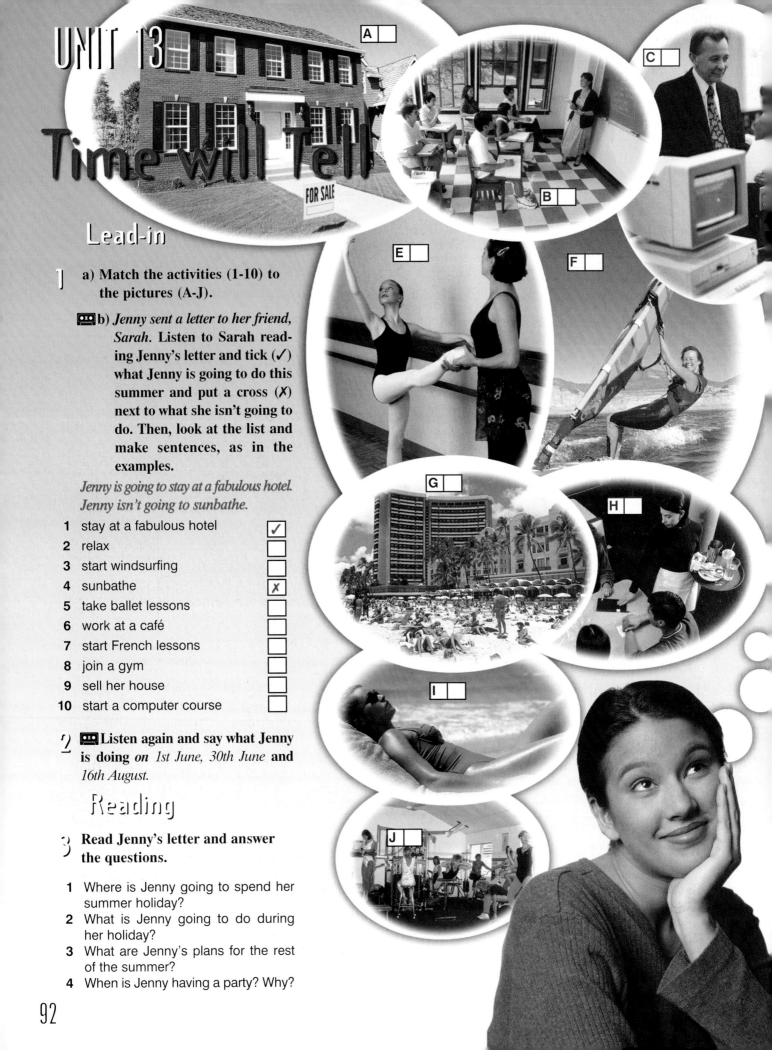

Lead-in

1 a) **Match the activities (1-10) to the pictures (A-J).**

📼 b) *Jenny sent a letter to her friend, Sarah.* **Listen to Sarah reading Jenny's letter and tick (✓) what Jenny is going to do this summer and put a cross (✗) next to what she isn't going to do. Then, look at the list and make sentences, as in the examples.**

Jenny is going to stay at a fabulous hotel. Jenny isn't going to sunbathe.

1	stay at a fabulous hotel	✓
2	relax	☐
3	start windsurfing	☐
4	sunbathe	✗
5	take ballet lessons	☐
6	work at a café	☐
7	start French lessons	☐
8	join a gym	☐
9	sell her house	☐
10	start a computer course	☐

2 📼 **Listen again and say what Jenny is doing on** *1st June, 30th June* **and** *16th August.*

Reading

3 **Read Jenny's letter and answer the questions.**

1 Where is Jenny going to spend her summer holiday?
2 What is Jenny going to do during her holiday?
3 What are Jenny's plans for the rest of the summer?
4 When is Jenny having a party? Why?

D

6 Greenway Road
Wethersham
6 May, ...

Dear Sarah,

I've got some great news. Richard and I are going on holiday for a whole month. Guess where — Hawaii!

We're leaving on 1st June. We both love swimming, so we're going to stay at a fabulous hotel right next to the beach. I'm going to relax as much as possible because I'm quite tired after working hard all this year.

We're coming back from our holidays on 30th June, and I've got lots of plans for the rest of the summer. First, I'm going to work at a café because I want to earn some extra money and buy a new car. I'm also going to join a gym to lose some weight. Finally, I want to find a better job in autumn, so I'm going to start a computer course.

Oh, I nearly forgot! On 16th August we're having a garden party to celebrate Richard's birthday. Please try to come. You're welcome to spend the night here.

Well, that's all for now. Hope to see you soon.

Love,
Jenny

• Speaking

Copy and complete the tables, then talk about Jenny's plans/intentions and arrangements. Use *because* or *to-inf* to join the sentences.

PLANS/INTENTIONS	REASON/PURPOSE
they/stay at ......*a hotel*......	they both love .*swimming*.
she/relax	she's quite ....
she/work	earn ....
she/join	lose ....
she/start	find ....

FIXED ARRANGEMENTS
they/leave on ....
they/come back .... on ....
they/have a .... on .... to ....

*They are going to stay at a hotel next to the beach **because** they both love swimming.*

Language Development

• Vocabulary

4 Choose words from the list to fill in the gaps, then use them to make sentences.

computer, great, go, earn, work, join, lose, fabulous

1	.... news	5	to .... money
2	to .... on holiday	6	to .... a gym
3	a .... hotel	7	to .... weight
4	to .... hard	8	a .... course

• Grammar: be going to

Expressing Plans and Intentions

Affirmative:	I **am**/You **are**/He **is**, etc **going to** move house.
Negative:	I'm **not**/You **aren't**/He **isn't**, etc **going to** move house.
Interrogative:	**Am** I/**Are** you/**Is** he, etc **going to** move house?
Short answers:	Yes, I **am**/you **are**/he **is**, etc. No, I'm **not**/ you **aren't**/he **isn't**, etc.

be going to - present continuous

We use **be going to** to talk about future plans and intentions. We use the **present continuous** to talk about fixed future arrangements.

plans/intentions be going to	fixed arrangements present continuous

I'm going to fly to Poland soon.	*I'm flying to Poland at 7 o'clock.*

5 Choose activities from the list and say three things you *are* going to do at the weekend, and three things you are *not* going to do.

stay at home, watch TV, meet my friends, have a party, play football, study for a test, fly to New Delhi, listen to music and relax, clean my room

I'm going to listen to music and relax.
I'm not going to fly to New Delhi.

6 **Look at Tom's arrangements, then, in pairs, ask and answer questions, as in the example.**

> **SATURDAY 4th JULY**
>
> 10 am: visit the dentist
> 11 am: meet Frank for coffee
> 1 pm: have lunch with Jane
> 5 pm: catch the train
> to London

SA: What is Tom doing at ten o'clock?
SB: He's **visiting the dentist** at ten o'clock.

be going to - present continuous

- We also use **be going to** for predictions based on evidence in the present.
- We also use the **present continuous** for actions happening now, at the moment of speaking.

be going to: evidence that something is going to happen

present continuous: action happening now

There are dark clouds in the sky. It's **going to** rain.

It's **raining**.

7 **Look at the pictures and the prompts. In pairs, ask and answer questions, as in the example. Finally, write a sentence about each picture.**

she/wash the car - he/have a bath - she/drink some orange juice - he/paint the house - they/play football

Picture 1: SA: What's she going to do?
SB: She's going to wash the car.
Picture 2: SA: What's she doing? ...

1 She's going to wash the car.

2 ....

3 ....

4 ....

5 ....

6 ....

7 ....

8 ....

9 ....

10 ....

• Game

In two teams, take it in turns to answer your teacher's questions. Each correct answer gets one point. The team with the most points is the winner.

Teacher: Look at picture 1. Is she washing the car?
Team A S1: No, she isn't. She's going to wash the car.

Expressing Reason, Result or Purpose

- We express reason with **because** and result with **so**.
- We also express reason or purpose with **to-infinitive** (infinitive of purpose).
  *She's going to join a gym **because** she wants to lose some weight.*
  *She wants to lose some weight, **so** she's going to join a gym.*
  *She's going to join a gym **to lose** some weight.*

8 Match Tony's intentions to his reasons, then make sentences, as in the examples.

Intentions	Reason/Purpose
1 save money	a keep fit
2 join a gym	b pass his exams
3 stop eating sweets	c go on holiday
4 study hard	d lose weight
5 learn English	e get a better job

*Tony is going to save money **because** he wants to go on holiday.*
*Tony wants to go on holiday, **so** he is going to save money.*
*Tony is going to save money **to go** on holiday.*

Will

We use **will**:
- to make predictions.
  *In 100 years' time, there **will be** underwater cities.*
- to make on-the-spot decisions.
  *I'll **have** soup first, then steak and chips.*

Time expressions used with future tenses: tomorrow, soon, next week/month/etc, the day after tomorrow, etc.

9 Read the examples and say:
a) which are predictions;
b) which are on-the-spot decisions.

1 I'm cold. I'll close the window.
2 In 50 years' time, I think there **will** be more cars in the streets than people.
3 It **will** be cold and rainy tomorrow.
4 I'm hungry. I'll make myself a sandwich.
5 In 100 years' time, people **will** have flying cars.

It will be - There will be

It will be + adjective: *It will be rainy tomorrow.*
There will be + noun: *There will be rain tomorrow.*

10 🔊 a) Look at the international weather chart and the symbols, then listen and tick (✓) the correct symbol. Finally make sentences, as in the examples.

It will be sunny in Bangkok tomorrow.
There will be sunshine in Bangkok tomorrow

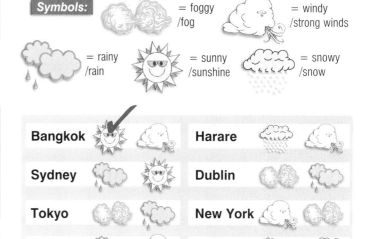

Symbols:
= foggy /fog
= windy /strong winds
= rainy /rain
= sunny /sunshine
= snowy /snow

Bangkok		Harare	
Sydney		Dublin	
Tokyo		New York	
Seoul		Warsaw	

b) In pairs, ask and answer questions, as in the example.

SA: Will it be sunny in Bangkok tomorrow?
SB: Yes, it will.
SA: Will it be sunny in Dublin tomorrow?
SB: No, it won't.

c) Fill in *There* or *It*.

1 .... will be foggy in Dublin tomorrow.
2 .... will be strong winds in Harare tomorrow.
3 .... will be rainy in Seoul tomorrow.
4 .... will be sunny in Sydney tomorrow.
5 .... will be snow in Warsaw tomorrow.

11 Read the prompts and match them to the correct on-the-spot decisions, then make sentences, as in the example.

	on-the-spot decisions
I'm thirsty.	close the window
It's raining.	have a sandwich
It's cold.	have a glass of water
I'm tired.	call the fire brigade
I'm hungry.	go to bed
It's hot.	open the window
The house is on fire.	put on my raincoat

I'm thirsty. I'll have a glass of water.

• Reading & Listening

12 a) **Which month were you born in? What is your star sign? Read the sentences, then listen to Madame Annette and write T (for true) or F (for false).**

Taurus: This will be a difficult week. ....
Cancer: You'll go on a short journey this week. ....
Leo: You'll get some good news in a letter. ....
Libra: This will be a bad week. ....
Capricorn: This won't be a good week for you. ....
Aquarius: This will be your lucky week. ....

b) **Read the horoscopes and answer the questions. For some questions, there is more than one correct answer. Finally, explain the words in bold.**

Which horoscope says:

1 you'll receive a letter from a friend? ...*Taurus*...........
2 you'll get an invitation/invitations? ....
3 you'll have health problems? ....
4 you'll get a lot of money?..
5 you'll have problems with someone in your family?......................................

Taurus (Apr. 20 - May 21)
This will be an **exciting** week. You'll **receive** a letter from a friend. At the weekend you'll get a special **invitation. Accept** it.

Gemini (May 22 - June 21)
This will be a difficult week. You'll **argue with** your best friend. Don't worry — you'll soon be friends again.

Cancer (June 22 - July 22)
You'll go on a long **journey** this week. You'll enjoy yourself a lot, but don't drive too fast.

Leo (July 23 - Aug. 23)
You'll get some good **news** in a letter, and you'll **have a lot of fun** on Saturday.

Virgo (Aug. 24 - Sept. 23)
You'll have problems with someone in your family. Don't worry — everything will be okay soon.

Libra (Sept. 24 - Oct. 23)
This will be a **pleasant** week. You'll go on a short **trip** and you'll have lots of fun.

Scorpio (Oct. 24 - Nov. 22)
You will lose some money on Tuesday. A friend will bring you some good news. You'll get an invitation at the weekend. Don't accept it.

Sagittarius (Nov. 23 - Dec. 21)
This will be a **horrible** week. There will be bad news on Wednesday and you'll have problems with someone in your family. The weekend will be better.

Capricorn (Dec. 22 - Jan. 20)
This won't be a good week for you. You'll have problems with your **health**. Try to relax.

Aquarius (Jan. 21 - Feb. 18)
This will be your **lucky** week. You will get a lot of money. You'll get an invitation at the weekend. Accept it.

Pisces (Feb. 19 - Mar. 20)
This will be a bad week. You will have problems with your health. Try to rest during the weekend. Things will be better next week.

Aries (Mar. 21 - Apr. 19)
It will be a pleasant week for you. You'll meet an interesting person and you'll get a lot of invitations. Enjoy yourself.

• Speaking

13 **Study the language key in the Photo File section, then ask your partner what his/her star sign is. Use the key to tell them their horoscope for next week.**

Writing (Project)

Use the information in the Photo File section to write next week's horoscopes. Decorate your project with the pictures of the star signs.

14 ▣ *What will life be like in 30 years' time?* **Read the sentences, then listen and put a *W* for the woman's predictions and a *M* for the man's.**

People will travel in flying cars.
People will live in underwater cities.
Life will be more expensive.
People will go on holiday to the moon.
There will be more people in the world.
Pollution will be worse.
There won't be enough trees.
People will use oxygen masks to breathe.
There will be food pills instead of fresh food.
There won't be enough water for everyone.

• Communication: Accepting and Refusing Invitations

15 ▣ **Listen to the dialogues. Who accepts an invitation? Who refuses an invitation? In pairs, use the prompts to act out similar dialogues.**

meet Jenny, go to the beach, play tennis with Claire, go to a disco, watch a play

a) A: What are you doing this Saturday, Cindy?
B: **I'm going to my cousin's birthday party.** Do you want to come with me?
A: I'd love to.

b) A: Are you doing anything this Saturday, Steve?
B: **I'm going to visit my parents.** Would you like to come with me?
A: I'd love to, but I can't. **I'm going to the cinema with Bob.**

Pronunciation

16 ▣ **Listen and tick. Listen again and repeat.**

	/h/ pronounced	/h/ silent
hour		
horrible		
vehicle		
honest		
hand		
perhaps		

• Vocabulary Revision Game

17 **Work in two teams. Take it in turns to choose words from the list and make sentences. Each correct sentence gets one point. The team with the most points is the winner.**

pollution, work hard, relax, horrible week, celebrate, soon, health problems, underwater cities, oxygen masks, breathe, food pills, better job, earn, have a lot of fun

Writing (a letter to a friend about your plans)

When we write **a letter to a friend about our plans**, we divide the letter into **four paragraphs**. We **start** with *Dear + our friend's first name*. In this type of letter we use **be going to** to talk about our plans/intentions and the **present continuous** to talk about fixed future arrangements. To express **reason** or **purpose**, we use **so**, **because** or **to-infinitive**. We **end** the letter with *Love/Best Wishes/Yours, + our first name*.

18 **Write a letter to a friend telling him/her about your plans and inviting him/her to your house for a special event. Use the plan below to help you, as well as the letter in Ex. 3.**

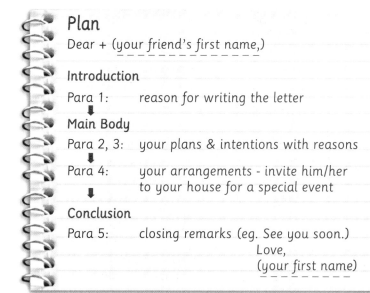

Plan
Dear + (your friend's first name,)

Introduction
Para 1:   reason for writing the letter
    ↓
Main Body
Para 2, 3:   your plans & intentions with reasons
    ↓
Para 4:   your arrangements - invite him/her
            to your house for a special event
    ↓
Conclusion
Para 5:   closing remarks (eg. See you soon.)
            Love,
            (your first name)

Words of Wisdom

Read these sentences. What do they mean?

• Time will tell.
• A change is as good as a rest.
• Tomorrow never comes.

UNIT 14

Dos and Don'ts

Lead-in

1
- **Read the statements a to e. Which refers to:**

  health?   house rules?   the environment?
  travel?   school?

  a Use buses and trams — not cars.

  b Always have your passport with you.

  c Eat lots of fruit and vegetables.

  d Don't keep pets in your room.

  e Never eat in class.

- **Can you think of any more *dos* and *don'ts* for each subject?**

2 **Look at the pictures. Find the picture which shows:**

1 pre-packaged food ....; **2** washing-up liquid ....;
3 an aluminium can ....; **4** a recycling bin ....;
5 public transport ....; **6** rubbish ....;
7 a forest ....; **8** plastic bottles ....;
9 an aerosol can ....; **10** a rubbish bin ....

Now, say what you can see in each picture, as in the example. *I can see a forest in picture A.*

3 **Listen and circle the correct item.**

1 a) Try not to buy pre-packaged food.
   b) Try to buy pre-packaged food.

2 a) Always light fires in forests.
   b) Never light fires in forests.

3 a) Do not throw plastic bottles into the sea.
   b) Throw plastic bottles into the sea.

4 a) Use aerosols.
   b) Do not use aerosols.

Reading

4 a) **Read the leaflet and match the instructions to the pictures on p. 98, then explain the words in bold.**

b) **Read the leaflet and find the reason for each instruction. In pairs, ask and answer questions, as in the example.**

SA: The leaflet says, "Try not to buy pre-packaged food." Why?

SB: Because the packaging creates a lot of rubbish.

HELPING THE ENVIRONMENT

*There are a lot of things we can do to **protect** the environment.*

- **Try** not to buy pre-packaged food. The packaging **creates** a lot of rubbish. ☐

- **Use less** washing-up liquid. It pollutes the seas and rivers. ☐

- Put aluminium cans into recycling bins. **Factories** can use them to **make** new things. ☐

- Use public transport (i.e. buses, trains, trams, etc). Cars pollute the air. ☐

- Never **light fires** in forests. Trees will **burn**. ☐

- Do not **drop** rubbish in the street. It **looks** and **smells** horrible. Use rubbish bins. ☐

- Do not **throw** plastic bottles into the sea. Fish will **die**. ☐

- Do not use aerosols. They pollute the air. ☐

Language Development

• Vocabulary

5 **Choose words from the list to fill in the gaps, then use them to make sentences.**

smells, aluminium, plastic, washing-up, pre-packaged, public, light, pollute

1 .... food
2 .... liquid
3 .... cans
4 .... transport
5 to .... the air
6 to .... fires
7 it .... horrible
8 .... bottles

Giving Instructions

We use the **imperative** to tell people what to do or not to do. *Use public transport. Do not use aerosols.*

• Speaking

Cover the leaflet, then look at the pictures on p. 98 and try to remember the dos and don'ts with their reasons, as they appeared in the leaflet.

• Grammar

Giving Advice

We use **should** to say what the right/best thing to do is.
*You **should** use public transport. (= It's a good idea.)*
We use **shouldn't** to say what isn't the right/best thing to do.
*You **shouldn't** use aerosols. (= It isn't a good idea.)*
We can also give advice with: ***Why don't you...? I think it's a good idea to ..., I don't think it's a good idea to ...***
***Why don't you** use public transport?*
***I think it's a good idea to** use public transport.*
***I don't think it's a good idea to** use aerosols.*

6 🔊 *Steve wants to keep fit and healthy.* **Look at the table, then listen to what his friend tells him. Tick (✓) the things he should do and put a cross (✗) next to the things he shouldn't do. Finally, use the expressions in the list to give advice to Steve.**

I (don't) think it's a good idea to ..., You should(n't) ..., Why don't you ...?

eat too many hamburgers or pizzas	
eat a lot of chocolate or ice-cream	
eat a lot of fruit and vegetables	
drink fizzy drinks or beer	
drink a lot of water	
have cereal with milk for breakfast	
take regular exercise	
walk to work	

I don't think it's a good idea to eat too many hamburgers or pizzas. OR
You shouldn't eat too many hamburgers or pizzas.

Writing (Project)

Steve sent a letter to his aunt asking for advice on how to keep fit and healthy. Look at the letter his aunt sent him in the Photo File section and write it out in full sentences.

• Reading & Listening

7 🔊 **a) Listen and circle the correct word in italics.**

1 In England, **always/never** ask before smoking in someone's house.
2 In China, never be **late/early** for appointments.
3 In Japan, leave your **gifts/shoes** at the door.

b) The statements from 1 to 12 are tips for visitors to England, China and Japan. Read the statements (1-12) and explain the words in bold, then guess which country each statement is for. Write J (for Japan), E (for England) or C (for China). Finally, read the texts and check your answers.

ENGLAND

The first thing you should remember when in England is always to say 'please' and 'thank you'. Never push into a queue of people or they'll get angry. Don't be late for appointments and don't talk with your mouth full. Remember — always ask before smoking in someone's house.

CHINA

When in China, don't kiss anyone in public — it's very rude. Never be late for appointments, and don't tell jokes to people you don't know very well. Be careful when you are eating, too — never leave your chopsticks pointing upwards in your rice because this makes people very upset. A last tip — when you give someone a present, give it with both hands.

When you visit someone in Japan, it is polite to take a gift. Remember to take your shoes off as you enter the house — they will give you special slippers to wear instead. Leave your shoes at the door, but make sure the toes are pointing towards the door. When you are in the living-room, don't sit anywhere you like — wait until someone shows you where to sit. Also, don't blow your nose in public — find a place where you can do it alone.

STATEMENTS

1 Ask before smoking in someone's house. ...*E*...
2 When you visit someone, take a **gift** with you. ....
3 **Take your shoes off** as you enter the house. ....
4 Don't **kiss** anyone **in public**. ....
5 Always say 'please' and 'thank you'. ....
6 Don't **blow your nose in public**. ....
7 Never leave your **chopsticks pointing upwards** in your rice. ....
8 Never **push into a queue** of people. ....
9 Make sure the **toes of your shoes** are pointing towards the door. ....
10 Don't be late for **appointments**. ...., ...
11 Don't tell **jokes** to people you don't know well. ....
12 Don't talk with your **mouth full**. ....

• Speaking

8 **What advice can you give to visitors to England, China and Japan? Give at least three pieces of advice for each country.**

When in England, you should say 'please' and 'thank you'.

9 a) **Fill in the gaps in the speech bubbles with the correct words from the list.**

flu, headache, toothache, cold, tired, sore throat

I've got a ....

1

I've got a ....

2

I feel very ....

3

I've got the ....

4

I feel very ....

5

I've got ....

6

b) **Match the pictures above to the best piece of advice in the list below.**

Take an aspirin. ....*1*...; Put a jumper on. ....; See the dentist. ....; Get some sleep. ....; Take some cough syrup. ....; Call the doctor and go to bed. ....

• Communication: Giving Advice

10 🔲 **Listen to the dialogues, then, in pairs, act out similar dialogues using the prompts from Ex. 9.**

A: Tony, what's the matter?
B: I've got a terrible headache.
A: Why don't you take an aspirin?

A: Bob, what's wrong with you?
B: I feel very tired.
A: You should get some sleep.

• Grammar

can/can't, must/mustn't

We use **can** to give permission.
*You **can** listen to the radio. (You are allowed to.)*

We use **can't** to refuse permission.
*You **can't** keep pets in your room. (You aren't allowed to.)*

We use **must** to tell someone to do something.
(expressing obligation)
*You **must** clean your room. (You are obliged to.)*

We use **mustn't** to tell someone not to do something.
(expressing prohibition)
*You **mustn't** smoke in hospitals. (It's forbidden.)*

11 🔲 **Listen to Mrs Battersby talking to her new lodger and put a tick (✓) in the correct column. Then, make sentences using *must, can't* or *can*.**

	MUST	CAN'T	CAN
keep pets		✓	
have parties in the room			
play loud music			
use the telephone			
have a TV in the room			
keep the room clean			
make the bed			
put posters on the walls			
pay the rent on time			
be home by 11 pm			

You can't keep pets.

• Speaking

12 **Work in pairs. Use the prompts in Ex. 11 and act out short dialogues, as in the examples.**

SA: Do I have to make the bed?
SB: Yes, you do. You must make the bed.

SA: Can I play loud music?
SB: No, you can't.

SA: Can I use the telephone?
SB: Yes, of course you can.

13 a) Look at the picture. Each student is doing something wrong. Use the prompts in the list to tell the students what they *must* or *mustn't* do while in class.

eat in class, chew gum in class, write on the walls, keep the classroom clean, be quiet in class, cheat in tests, sleep in class, talk to each other in class, bring pets into school, fight in class
1-You **mustn't** *eat in class.*

b) Make three rules for your school. Use *must* or *mustn't*.
You **must** *do your homework.*

Pronunciation

14 🎧 Listen and tick. Listen again and repeat.

	/ r / pronounced	/ r / silent
turn		
care		
hurry		
various		

• Vocabulary Revision Game

15 Work in two teams. Take it in turns to choose words from the list and make sentences. Each correct sentence gets one point. The team with the most points is the winner.

pre-packaged food, pollute, protect, recycling bins, light fires, it's a good idea to, keep fit, blow your nose, queue, with your mouth full, tell jokes, appointments

• Communication

16 🎧 Read the short dialogues and fill in *must, mustn't, can, can't, should* or *shouldn't*, then listen and check your answers. Finally, in pairs, act out similar dialogues.

a) giving advice

A: I can't see that sign very well.
B: You .... see an optician.

A: I feel tired.
B: You .... go to bed so late.

b) giving permission

A: .... I use your phone, please?
B: Yes, of course you ....

c) expressing obligation

A: Do I have to wash the dishes?
B: Yes, you do! You .... wash the dishes — it's your turn!

d) refusing permission

A: Mum, ... I have some sweets?
B: No, you .... They're bad for your teeth.

e) expressing prohibition

A: Can I park here?
B: No, you can't. You .... park here — it's illegal.

17 a) **Match the pictures to the instructions, then expand them into full sentences. Use** *always,* *never* **or** *don't.*

b) **Match the instructions to the reasons.**

 C
 D
 A
 B
 E
 F

G

Instructions

- A put suncream on/skin
- drop litter on/beach
- play in/sun between 11am & 3pm
- wear/hat
- swim after eating
- wear sunglasses
- swim near windsurfers

Reasons

The sun is very dangerous then.

It protects your skin from the hot sun.

It protects your head from the sun.

There is always a danger of accidents.

It looks and smells horrible.

It is dangerous to swim with a full stomach.

They protect your eyes from the sun.

Writing (a leaflet giving advice)

When we write **leaflets** giving rules, regulations, advice, instructions, etc, we write **one rule after the other** on separate lines. We use the **imperative** and words like *never, always, make sure*, etc. We may also give the reason why we should do what the rule says.
Never light fires in forests. Trees will burn.

Write a leaflet giving advice to people on what to do while they are on the beach during the summer (50 - 80 words). Use ideas from Ex. 17, as well as your own ideas. Start like this:

ENJOY THE SEA AND SUN

Summer is here. It's holiday time. Pack your things and head for the nearest beach. But keep in mind the following useful tips.

Words of Wisdom

Read these sentences. What do they mean?

- When in Rome, do as the Romans do.
- Experience is the best teacher.

UNIT 15

Take a Break

Lead-in

1 Look at the pictures. Which country are they from? Have you ever been there? If so, when and why?

2 Which picture shows:

a a Pyramid?
b the Sphinx?
c a man on a camel?
d museum exhibits?
e the Khan al-Khalili bazaar?
f a boat on the River Nile?
g a Pharaoh's mask?
h statues of lions?

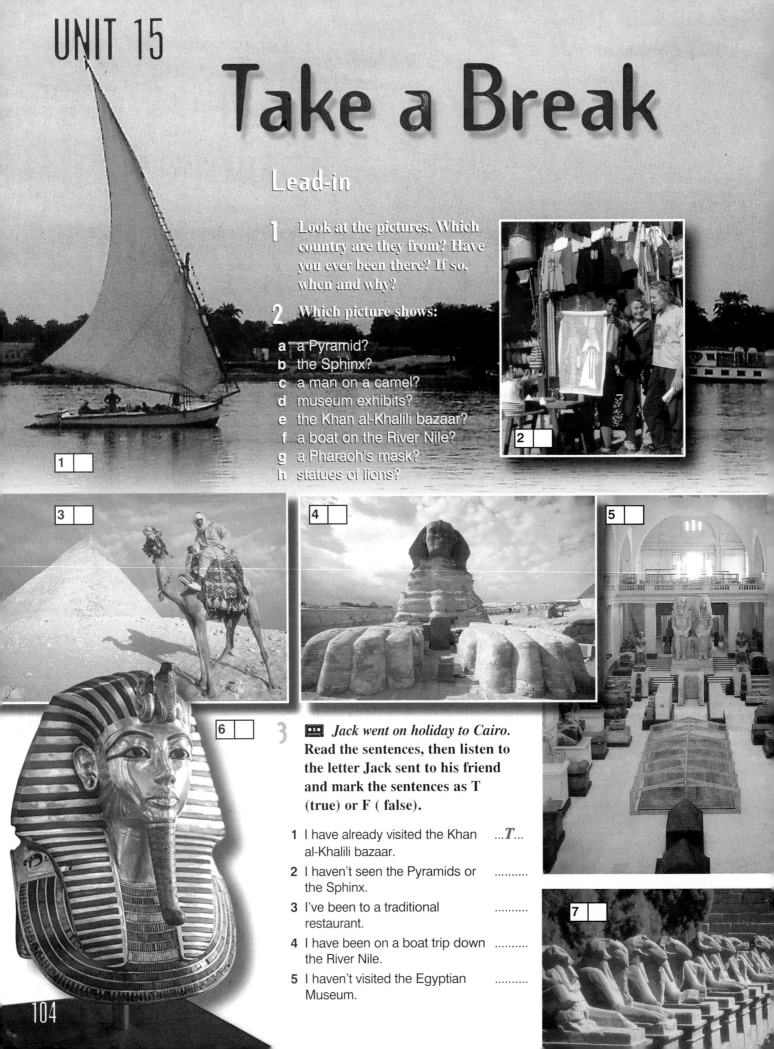

3 🔊 *Jack went on holiday to Cairo. Read the sentences, then listen to the letter Jack sent to his friend and mark the sentences as T (true) or F (false).*

1 I have already visited the Khan al-Khalili bazaar. ...*T*...

2 I haven't seen the Pyramids or the Sphinx. ....

3 I've been to a traditional restaurant. ....

4 I have been on a boat trip down the River Nile. ....

5 I haven't visited the Egyptian Museum. ....

Reading

4 **Read the letter and underline the sentences which match pictures 4 and 7, then answer the questions.**

Dear Terry,

Greetings from Cairo! The weather is very hot here and I'm having a wonderful time. I'm staying with my friend, Abdullah. He lives in the centre of Cairo.

I've been here since Monday and I've already done lots of things! I've already visited the Khan al-Khalili bazaar. We visited it on Tuesday. You can't imagine how noisy and crowded it was! I bought some lovely handmade souvenirs there. I have also seen the Pyramids and the Sphinx at Giza. I saw them yesterday. They were amazing. I even rode a camel. It was fun! I've been to a traditional restaurant. Abdullah took me there last night. I tried couscous and falafel. The place was fantastic and the food was just delicious.

There are a lot of things I haven't done yet. I haven't been on a boat trip down the River Nile yet, and I haven't visited the Egyptian Museum. We are going on a boat trip tomorrow and we are going to visit the museum one of these days to see the exhibits. We are also going to visit Luxor. The place is famous for its huge temples and statues.

Cairo is a fascinating city — you must visit it one day! Anyway, I'm returning to England on Sunday next week, so I'll call you then.

Best wishes,
Jack

1 Where is Jack?
2 What is the weather like there?
3 Who is Jack staying with?
4 How long has Jack been there?
5 What did Jack do on Tuesday?
6 What did he do yesterday?
7 What hasn't he done yet?
8 What is he going to do before he leaves?
9 When is he returning to England?
10 What does he think of the place?

• Speaking

Read the letter again, then copy the table and complete it. In pairs, ask and answer questions, as in the example.

HAS	WHEN	WHAT IT WAS LIKE	WHAT HE DID THERE
visited the Khan al-Khalili bazaar	Tuesday	noisy & crowded	bought souvenirs

SA: *Has Jack visited the Khan al-Khalili bazaar?*
SB: *Yes, he has.*
SA: *When did he visit it?*
SB: *On Tuesday.*
SA: *What was it like?*
SB: *It was noisy and crowded.*
SA: *What did he do there?*
SB: *He bought some souvenirs.*

Language Development

• Vocabulary

5 **Choose words from the list to fill in the gaps, then use them to make sentences.**

rode, handmade, fascinating, centre, huge, boat, traditional, wonderful

1 .... temples
2 having a .... time
3 in the .... of Cairo
4 .... restaurant
5 .... souvenirs
6 a .... trip
7 I .... a camel
8 a .... city

6 **Replace the adjectives in bold with their opposites.**

disgusting, cold, quiet, horrible, empty, modern

1 I'm having a **wonderful** time.
2 The streets are **noisy** and **crowded**.
3 We've been to a **traditional** restaurant.
4 The food was **delicious**.
5 The weather is very **hot**.

7 **Fill in the missing prepositions, then use them to make sentences.**

for, down, on, with, at

1 I'm staying ...... my friend; 2 ...... Tuesday; 3 ...... Giza;
4 go ...... a boat trip ...... the River Nile; 5 famous ......

• Grammar: Present Perfect (have/has + past participle)

8 Complete the table, then study the rules.

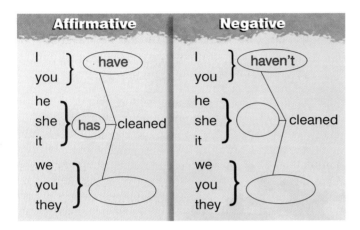

Affirmative	Negative
I / you } **have**	I / you } **haven't**
he / she / it } **has** — cleaned	he / she / it } ◯ — cleaned
we / you / they } ◯	we / you / they } ◯

Present Perfect - Past Simple

• We form the present perfect with **have/has** and the **past participle** of the main verb.
• We use the **present perfect** to talk about an action which happened in the past, without saying when it happened. *He's been to Spain. (We don't know when he went to Spain.)*
• We use the **past simple** to talk about an action which happened at a definite time in the past. *He went to Spain last month. (When did he go to Spain? Last month. - definite time)*
• **Time adverbs used with the present perfect**: *ever, just, yet, already, for, since, etc.*
• **Time adverbs used with the past simple**: *yesterday, two/ three/etc days/months/etc ago, last Monday/week/ month, etc.*

9 Read the letter in Ex. 4 and find three things Jack *has* done and two things Jack *hasn't* done.

10 Complete the short answers in the table.

Interrogative	Short answers
Have I/we/you/they **been** to Turkey?	Yes, I/we/you/they .... No, I/we/you/they ....
Has he/she/it **been** to Turkey?	Yes, he/she/it .... No, he/she/it ....

Present Perfect + Ever/Never

• We use **ever** in questions and statements. *Have you **ever** visited Brazil? Brazil is the best place I've **ever** visited.*
• We use **never** in statements. *I've **never** visited Cyprus. I haven't visited Cyprus.*

11 Look at the countries, then make sentences, as in the examples.

Australia	Turkey	Greece

Mexico	Italy	Canada	Spain

Poland	Brazil	China

*I've been to Spain. It's the best country I've **ever** visited.*
*I've **never** been to China.*

12 In pairs, use the prompts and the adjectives in the list to ask and answer questions, as in the examples.

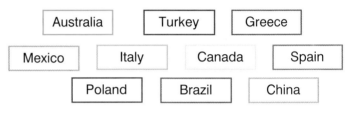

• visit Prague? - last summer
• ride a camel? - no
• stay in a big hotel? - last winter
• eat Chinese food? - last Sunday
• meet a famous person? - no
• drive a bus? - no
• fly in a plane? - a month ago

adjectives: *exciting, fantastic, amazing, delicious, great, awful, horrible, terrible, disgusting*

SA: *Have you ever visited Prague?*
SB: *Yes, I have.*
SA: *When did you visit Prague?*
SB: *Last summer. It was exciting.*

SA: *Have you ever ridden a camel?*
SB: *No, I haven't. I've never ridden a camel.*

Present Perfect + Yet/Already

• We use **already** in positive statements.
• We use **yet** in questions and negatives. *Have you packed your suitcase **yet**?* **No, I haven't. I haven't** packed it **yet**. **Yes, I have. I've already** packed it.

13 📼 *Tony and Ann are in Paris on holiday.* **Look at the table, then listen and tick (✓) the activities that they have already done and put a cross (✗) next to those that they haven't done yet. Finally, in pairs, ask and answer questions, as in the example.**

SA: *Have they visited the Eiffel Tower **yet**?*
SB: *Yes, they have **already** visited the Eiffel Tower. Have they been to Versailles **yet**?*
SA: *No, they haven't been to Versailles **yet**.*

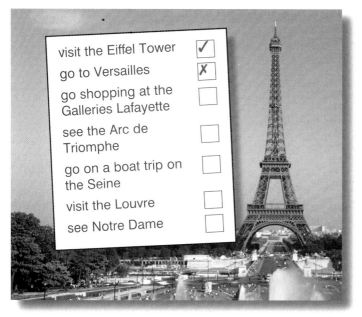

visit the Eiffel Tower	✓
go to Versailles	✗
go shopping at the Galleries Lafayette	☐
see the Arc de Triomphe	☐
go on a boat trip on the Seine	☐
visit the Louvre	☐
see Notre Dame	☐

Present Perfect + Just

- We use **just** in statements to show that an action finished only a few minutes earlier.
  A: Have you packed your suitcase yet?
  *B: Yes, I've **just** packed it.*

14 **Work in pairs. Use the prompts to ask and answer questions with *yet* and *just*, as in the example.**

SA: *Have you booked a table **yet**?*
SB: *Yes, I've **just** booked it.*

1 book a table
2 pack our swimming costumes
3 find the tickets
4 talk to the receptionist
5 meet Steve

Present Perfect + For/Since

- We use **for** to express duration.
  *I've been here **for** five days.*
- We use **since** to state a starting point.
  *I've been here **since** Monday.*

15 **Expand the notes into sentences using *for* or *since*.**

1 He/be in Cairo/Friday *He has been in Cairo **since** Friday.*
2 He/live in Rome/three years
3 I/not see/Jane/ten years
4 I/not travel/by plane/1987
5 They/be/on holiday/last Monday

16 📼 **a) Listen and follow the dialogue, then read it and put the verbs in brackets into the correct tense. Listen again and check.**

Paul: Hello, Peter. What a surprise to meet you here in Madrid.
Peter: Hey, Paul! Fancy meeting you here. This place is fantastic.
Paul: Yes, it is. How long **1)** .... **(you/be)** here?
Peter: Oh, I **2)** .... **(arrive)** last Saturday. I **3)** .... **(stay)** at the Monaco Hotel. Where **4)** .... **(you/stay)**?
Paul: With my friend Carlos. I **5)** .... **(be)** here since last Monday.
Peter: Which places **6)** .... **(you/visit)**?
Paul: Well, I **7)** .... **(already/visit)** the Prado Museum. I **8)** .... **(go)** there last Monday. It's fantastic. I **9)** .... **(see)** some beautiful paintings there. You really should go.
Peter: I will, indeed. **10)** .... **(you/go)** to Palacio Real yet?
Paul: Yes, I **11)** .... **(go)** there yesterday. The state rooms were magnificent.
Peter: That sounds nice. **12)** .... **(you/be)** shopping at all?
Paul: No, I haven't, but I **13)** .... **(do)** that soon. I **14)** .... **(want)** to go to the Rastro flea market to buy some souvenirs.
Peter: That's a good idea. **15)** .... **(you/try)** paella yet?
Paul: Of course. I **16)** .... **(go)** to 'Lhardy' restaurant last night with some friends. The food was just delicious.
Peter: I see you don't waste your time. What **17)** .... **(you/do)** tonight? Shall we go out for a drink?
Paul: I'd love to, but I can't. I **18)** .... **(go)** to the opera to see *Carmen*. But we can meet tomorrow.
Peter: Okay, then. How about 7 o'clock at Bistro Café?
Paul: All right. See you tomorrow.
Peter: See you.

b) Answer the questions.
1 Where is Paul?
2 When did he arrive?
3 Where is he staying?
4 What places has he visited?
5 What hasn't he done yet?
6 Where is he going tonight?

Writing (Project)

Use the information from Ex. 16 to write the letter Paul wrote to a friend while he was in Madrid.

• Reading & Listening

17 **a) Read the sentences, then listen and underline the correct words in bold.**

1 **Americans / Canadians** take tipping more seriously than any other nationality.
2 Tip your **bellboy / travel agent** generously, and you'll have the perfect holiday.
3 For tips of **$60 / $20** or more, your bellboy will be your friend forever.

b) Read the text below and choose the best answer to the questions that follow, then explain the words in bold.

TIPPING IN AMERICA

Americans take **tipping** more seriously than any other **nationality**, and of all Americans, no one takes tipping as seriously as hotel bellboys do.

Tip your bellboy **generously**, and you'll have the perfect holiday. Don't tip him, and you'll have the worst holiday of your life!

Guests who don't tip well at hotels often find that the **heating** in their room 'accidentally' stops working in the middle of winter, or that they **receive** strange phone calls in the middle of the night. Sometimes the keys for their room '**disappear**' and it seems that no one can find the **spare** keys.

It's a good idea to tip a bellboy at least $5 and, for tips of $20 or more, your bellboy will be your friend forever. So, anyone who is planning to stay in an American hotel should remember — bellboys can make sure you have the holiday of your dreams ... or they can make your visit a **nightmare**!

1 What happens to people who don't tip bellboys in the USA?
   A They will have a great holiday.
   B The bellboys will like them.
   C They will have a very bad holiday.

2 Which of the following can happen to guests who don't tip well?
   A Their heating goes off in the middle of winter.
   B They get more keys for their room.
   C They don't get any phone calls.

3 It's a good idea to tip a bellboy at least ...
   A $50.
   B $15.
   C $5.

4 Bellboys can make sure you have....
   A a cheap or an expensive holiday.
   B a good or a bad holiday.
   C a clean or a dirty room.

• Communication

18 **Listen to the three short dialogues and decide who is: a)** *making a reservation at a restaurant;* **b)** *inviting somebody out;* **c)** *buying souvenirs.* **In pairs, act out the dialogues.**

1 A: Hello, Rachel. What are you doing tonight?
   B: I haven't got any plans. Why?
   A: Well, there's a good film on at the Odeon tonight. Would you like to go?
   B: Yes — that would be great!
   A: Okay. I'll pick you up at eight, then.

2 A: Can I help you?
   B: Yes, please. I'm looking for a gift to take home for my brother.
   A: How about this wallet? It's a lovely gift for a man.
   B: How much is it?
   A: It's only £10.
   B: Great — I'll take it. I'm sure he'll like it.

3 A: Hello. I'd like to book a table for tonight, please.
   B: Certainly, madam. What time and for how many?
   A: A table for two at nine o'clock, please.
   B: That's fine. Could I have your name, please?
   A: Powers. Ann Powers.
   B: Thank you, Ms Powers. We'll see you tonight.

19 🎦 You are going to listen to some short exchanges. a) Read the possible responses, then listen and choose the best answer. b) Listen again and check your answers.

1 a) I'd love to.   b) I like it.

2 a) Two weeks ago.   b) Since Monday.

3 a) Yes, I can.   b) Yes, please.

4 a) Yes, I loved it.   b) Yes, I loved.

5 a) Yes, you have.   b) Yes, you do.

6 a) You must.   b) Of course.

7 a) In the spring.   b) Cairo.

8 a) Yes, I have.   b) Yes, I tried.

9 a) I won't.   b) That's a good idea.

10 a) Sorry, you can't.   b) No, you shouldn't.

11 a) Yes, you do.   b) Sorry, you mustn't.

12 a) Of course you can't. b) Of course you can.

• Vocabulary Revision Game

20 Work in two teams. Take it in turns to choose words from the list and make sentences. Each correct sentence gets one point. The team with the most points is the winner.

camel, since, have visited, souvenirs, traditional, returning, drive, yet, already, tip, bellboy, book a table

Pronunciation

21 🎦 Listen and tick. Listen again and repeat.

	/ ʃ /	/ tʃ /
shoes		
choose		
watch		
wash		

	/ ʃ /	/ tʃ /
wish		
witch		
sheet		
cheat		

Writing (a friendly letter from a holiday destination reporting your experiences)

When we are on holiday and we want to write to a friend to report our experiences, we **start** by saying **where we are**, **when we arrived** there, **what the weather** is like, and **where we are staying**.

Then, we talk about the **things we have** or **haven't done** (present perfect), **when we did them** and **what each was like** (past simple). We also say **what we are going to do**.

We **end** the letter by saying **what we think of the place** and **when we are leaving**.

Imagine you are on holiday. Use the plan below to write a letter to a friend telling him/her about your holiday (80 - 120 words). Use the letter in Ex. 4 as a model.

Plan

Dear + (your friend's first name,)

Introduction

Para 1: Where are you?
         When did you arrive there?
         What is the weather like?
         Where are you staying?

Main Body

Para 2: What things have you done?
         When did you do them?
         What was each like?

Para 3: What haven't you done yet?
         What are you going to do?

Conclusion

Para 4: What do you think of the place?
         When are you leaving?

                Best wishes/Love, etc
                (your first name)

Words of Wisdom

Read these sentences. What do they mean?

- He travels fastest who travels alone.
- Travel broadens the mind.

Strange Visitors

It's 9 pm on a January evening. The night is warm and dry. Sandra and David are in a jeep. They are driving through the fields near Myrrhee in Australia. They are doing some research to write a story about UFOs.

1 Look at the pictures on p. 110, then read the sentences and circle the correct answers.

1 Sandra and David are ....
A on a train   B in a jeep

2 It's 9 o'clock ....
A in the evening   B in the morning

3 Suddenly, Sandra and David see a .... in the sky.
A star   B bright light

4 It is a(n) ....
A spaceship   B aeroplane

2 Who asked the following? First, read the questions, then listen and write S (for Sandra) or D (for David).

1 Why are you slowing down?   ....
2 What on earth is going on?   ....
3 What is that bright light?   ....
4 What are those flashing lights?   ....

3 Read the episode and answer the questions.

1 What time of the year is it?
2 What is the weather like?
3 Where are Sandra and David?
4 Why are they there?
5 What does Sandra hear?
6 Where is it coming from?

4 Which of these phrases are related to the spaceship?

small, warm and dry, bright light, huge, flashing lights, noise, good-looking, patient, land

5 Fill in the correct word from the list.

look, believe, start, stand, wasting, no use, land

1 Many people .... in UFOs.
2 I can't .... this noise.
3 What's wrong with the car? I can't .... it.
4 Don't cry. It's ....
5 I think we are .... our time.
6 People say that UFOs .... in Myrrhee.
7 What does it .... like?

6 Listen to the episode and follow the dialogue. In pairs, read it out.

7 Look at the picture and label the parts of the jeep with words from the list. Then, describe the jeep.

bumper, steering wheel, headlight, windscreen, rear-view mirror, bonnet, wing mirror, seat, wheel

a ....   b ....
c ....   d ....
e ....
f ....   g ....
h ....
i ....

8 Read the summary and fill in the missing prepositions from the list.

down, through, of, in, into, near

David and Sandra are driving **1)** .... the fields **2)** .... Myrrhee in Australia. David does not believe **3)** .... UFOs and he thinks there is a logical explanation. Suddenly the jeep slows **4)** .... and David can't start it again.

Then Sandra sees a bright light **5)** .... the sky. It is a spaceship. David asks Sandra to take pictures **6)** .... the huge spaceship. David can't see anything because of the flashing lights and Sandra can't stand the noise. They are scared because the visitors are taking them **7)** .... the spaceship.

9 Read the list of events and put them in the correct order.

☐ The visitors are taking them into the spaceship.
☐ Sandra hears a noise.
☐1 David and Sandra are driving through the fields near Myrrhee.
☐ Sandra takes pictures.
☐ They see a bright light in the sky.

10 What do you think will happen to David and Sandra?

111

Strange Visitors

INSIDE THE SPACESHIP ...

What is it?

It is a female human.

And this here is a male human.

And what was that metal box they were in?

They call it a car. Very primitive means of transport.

We have studied similar humans before. They are still very primitive. They will not be able to understand our technology.

They are not ready to join us. Erase their memories and send them back.

SOME HOURS LATER IN THE JEEP...

What's wrong with this car, David?

I don't know. ... Ah! It's okay. It's started now!

That's strange. The film is full of pictures. Did we take any? I don't remember. Do you?

No, I don't, but I can see the camera is on automatic. Let's develop the film and see what's in it.

IN THE HOTEL ...

Sandra, you won't believe this.

What? A spaceship? Aliens? But how? When? What happened?

My dear Sandra, I can't answer these questions, but there is one thing I'm sure about. This is going to be our best story.

1 a) **Look at the pictures on p. 112, then read the statements and mark them as T (true) or F (false).**

1 There are three aliens inside the spaceship. ☐
2 The aliens have got long curly hair. ☐
3 The aliens are wearing long robes. ☐
4 David and Sandra are in the spaceship in the last picture. ☐

b) **Look at the last picture on p. 112. Why are David and Sandra surprised?**

2 🔊 **Read the sentences. The words in bold are opposites. Explain them, then listen and underline the correct word.**

1 And this here is a male **human/alien.**
2 Very **modern/primitive** means of transport.
3 They are not ready to **join/leave** us.
4 **Bring back/Erase** their memories.
5 The film is **empty/full of** pictures.
6 This is going to be our **best/worst** story.

3 **Read the episode and answer the questions.**

1 What is the "metal box" that the alien mentions?
2 Why do the aliens decide to erase David's and Sandra's memories?
3 What can't humans understand?
4 Why does David want to develop the film?
5 What do the pictures show?

4 **Match the sentences, then underline the correct linking word.**

1 David and Sandra are driving near Myrrhee
2 The jeep slows down,
3 They see a spaceship
4 The aliens take them into the spaceship
5 The aliens think David and Sandra are very primitive,
6 David finds the film is full of pictures,
7 They are surprised when they see the pictures

a **but/because** they want to study them
b **so/but** he doesn't remember using the camera
c **because/when** they want to write a story about UFOs.
d **but/so** they erase their memories and send them back.
e **so/but** Sandra and David don't know why.
f **because/and** they are pictures of aliens and a spaceship.
g **so/because** David asks Sandra to take some pictures.

5 **Label the pictures with the words below. Which of these means of transport are primitive and which are modern?**

cart, aeroplane, train, car, donkeys, camel, rowing boat, raft, hot air balloon

1 .... 2 .... 3 ....

4 .... 5 .... 6 ....

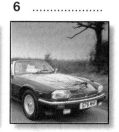

7 .... 8 .... 9 ....

6 🔊 **Listen to the episode and follow the dialogue, then read it out.**

7 **Fill in the correct form of the verbs in brackets.**

Myrrhee **1)** .... **(be)** a small place near the town of Moyhu in New South Wales, Australia. Many people **2)** .... **(say)** they **3)** .... **(see)** UFOs in the area, but the big question **4)** .... **(be)** this — why **5)** .... **(aliens/be)** interested in Myrrhee?

In the late 1960's, Erich von Däniken **6)** .... **(compare)** some ancient Aboriginal rock paintings to modern descriptions of aliens. They **7)** .... **(suggest)** that the ancient Aborigines **8)** .... **(know)** about aliens. Another interesting point **9)** .... **(be)** that many Aborigines **10)**................... **(live)** around the area of Myrrhee before the white man **11)**................. **(arrive)** in the 18th century. **12)** .... **(they/know)** about aliens? **13)** .... **(aliens/try)** to contact the Aborigines again? Unfortunately, we **14)** .... **(not/know)** for sure. One thing **15)** .... **(be)** certain, though — the truth **16)** .... **(be)** still out there ...

* *Aborigines - the original people of Australia*

113

• Vocabulary

1 Underline the correct word or phrase.

1 Yesterday we visited a *famous*/*public* temple.
2 You should always *tip*/*gift* bellboys in the USA.
3 In the year 2050 there will be *food pills*/*oxygen masks* instead of fresh food.
4 A lot of factories today use old *pre-packaged food*/*aluminium cans* to make new things.
5 When I was in London I *went*/*rode* on a boat trip.
6 "Did you have a good time at the museum?" "No, it was noisy and *pleasant*/*crowded*."
7 We bought some *handmade*/*clean* souvenirs.
8 You shouldn't *talk*/*kiss* anyone in public in China.
9 You mustn't *light*/*burn* fires in the forest.
10 We had dinner at a *traditional*/*delicious* restaurant last night.

(10 marks)

2 Use the words/phrases below to fill in the gaps.

ballet lessons, a wonderful time, tell jokes, headache, join a gym, drop, public transport, washing-up liquid

1 We should use less .... to help protect the environment.
2 I've got a terrible .... I'll take an aspirin.
3 "I want to keep fit." "Why don't you .... ?"
4 We had .... in Portugal.
5 I don't think it's a good idea to .... to people you don't know in China.
6 Mary is taking .... because she wants to become a ballerina.
7 Do not .... rubbish in the street — use a rubbish bin instead.
8 My father usually travels by ....

(10 marks)

3 Use the prepositions below to fill in the gaps.

with, to, at, on, for, in, from, into

1 You should never be late .... appointments.
2 My sister is flying .... Toronto .... 8 o'clock.
3 I live .... the city centre.
4 "Don't talk .... your mouth full, Tom."
5 You mustn't throw plastic bottles .... the sea.
6 They came back .... their holidays a week ago.
7 You will go .... a short journey this week.
8 Alex and Jo are going .... holiday .... a whole month.

(8 marks)

4 Use the words below to fill in the gaps. Then, use the phrases to write sentences, as in the example.

chew, short, pre-packaged, find, huge, sore, earn, great

1 to .... a better job
2 .... news
3 to .... money
4 a .... trip
5 .... food
6 to .... gum
7 a .... throat
8 .... temples

John wants to find a better job.

(8 marks)

• Grammar

5 Complete the table below with the past simple and past participles of the verbs.

	Infinitive	Past Simple	Past Participle
1	be	....	....
2	buy	....	bought
3	call	called	....
4	do	....	....
5	go	....	gone
6	have	....	....
7	live	....	....
8	return	returned	....
9	see	....	....
10	spend	....	spent
11	stay	....	....
12	take	took	....
13	visit	....	....
14	want	....	wanted

(7 marks)

6 Correct the mistakes.

1 Karen has lived here **for** 1989. ....
2 Tim is going to work at the supermarket in the holidays **so** he wants to earn extra money. ....
3 There aren't **some** clouds in the sky. I don't think it's going to rain. ....
4 **There** will be snowy in Montreal tomorrow. ....
5 When **have you visited** the museum? ....
6 You **must** smoke in hospitals. ....
7 Sharon **hasn't never travelled** by plane. ....
8 You **should** use aerosols. They pollute the air. ....
9 **Has you sent** the invitations yet? ....
10 They **have gone** to the zoo yesterday. ....
11 Mum, **must** I have an ice-cream, please? ....
12 He **cooks** dinner at the moment. ....

(12 marks)

7 Underline the correct word.

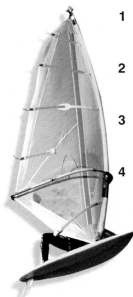

1 I haven't been windsurfing **since/for** a month.
2 We went on a boat trip two weeks **last/ago**.
3 Maria has **never/ever** played football.
4 A: Has Peter washed the car **yet/just**?
   B: Yes, he has He's **just/yet** finished.

(4 marks)

• Communication

8 Complete the dialogue with the questions below.

Would you like to go?
What are you doing tonight?

A: Hello, Helen. **1)** ....
....
B: I haven't got any plans. Why?
A: Well, there's a great concert on at the Royal Palace tonight. **2)** ....
....
B: Yes — that would be great!
A: Okay. I'll pick you up at seven, then.

(2 marks)

9 Use the verbs below to fill in the gaps.

can, can't, should, mustn't

A: I have got the flu.
B: You **1)** .... see a doctor.

A: Mum, **2)** .... I have a glass of milk, please?
B: Yes, of course you **3)** ....

A: Can I feed the animals?
B: No, you **4)** .... You **5)** .... feed the animals — it's forbidden.

(4 marks)

• Reading

10 First put the verbs in brackets into the correct tense, then correct the statements.

Dear Sam,
    Greetings from London! The weather **1)** .... **(be)** warm and sunny and I **2)** .... **(have)** a wonderful time. I **3)** .... **(stay)** with my Uncle Douglas. He **4)** .... **(live)** in the city centre.
    I **5)** .... **(already/visit)** Buckingham Palace. We **6)** .... **(visit)** it on Friday. I **7)** .... **(buy)** some postcards there. I **8)** .... **(also/go)** to Harrods. My uncle **9)** .... **(take)** me there yesterday, but I **10)** .... **(not/buy)** anything. I **11)** .... **(eat)** at an Indian restaurant too! We **12)** .... **(go)** there last night and I **13)** .... **(have)** a very hot curry!
    There are a lot of things I **14)** .... **(not/do)** yet. I **15)** .... **(not/go)** to Covent Garden or Piccadilly Circus yet. We **16)** .... **(go)** to Hyde Park tomorrow. London is a fascinating city — you must visit it one day! Anyway, I **17)** .... **(return)** home on 15th June, so I **18)** .... **(call)** you then.
    Best wishes,
    Ann

1 The weather in London is rainy.
2 Ann is having a terrible time.
3 Ann hasn't visited Buckingham Palace yet.
4 Ann bought lots of things in Harrods.
5 Ann's uncle took her to a traditional restaurant.
6 Ann and her uncle are going to Covent Garden tomorrow.
7 Ann is returning home on 20th August.

(20 marks)

Writing

11 Use the prompts below to complete Helen's letter to her friend, Pam.

14, Scott Road
Romley
8th June, ...

Dear Pam,

Para 1: Guess what! I/go/on holiday/with/friend/Claire/whole month!

Para 2: We/fly/Spain/20th June. Claire/I/love/climbing/so/we/stay/hotel/ near/the Pyrenees. We/want/travel/around Spain/too/so/we/ hire/car.

Para 3: We/come/back/from/holidays/21st July/I/have got/lots of plans/autumn. First/I/start/exercising/because/I/want/lose some weight. I/join/art class/learn/how/paint, too.

Para 4: Oh!/I/nearly/forget!/On 30th July/I/have a party/my house. Please/try/come. You/can/spend/night/here.

Para 5: Well/that/be/all/for now. Hope/see/you/soon.

Love,
Helen

(15 marks)

Irregular Verbs

Infinitive	Past	Past Participle
be	was	been
bear	bore	born(e)
beat	beat	beaten
become	became	become
begin	began	begun
bite	bit	bitten
blow	blew	blown
break	broke	broken
bring	brought	brought
build	built	built
burn	burnt (burned)	burnt (burned)
burst	burst	burst
buy	bought	bought
can	could	(been able to)
catch	caught	caught
choose	chose	chosen
come	came	come
cost	cost	cost
cut	cut	cut
deal	dealt	dealt
dig	dug	dug
do	did	done
dream	dreamt (dreamed)	dreamt (dreamed)
drink	drank	drunk
drive	drove	driven
eat	ate	eaten
fall	fell	fallen
feed	fed	fed
feel	felt	felt
fight	fought	fought
find	found	found
flee	fled	fled
fly	flew	flown
forbid	forbade	forbidden
forget	forgot	forgotten
forgive	forgave	forgiven
freeze	froze	frozen
get	got	got
give	gave	given
go	went	gone
grow	grew	grown
hang	hung (hanged)	hung (hanged)
have	had	had
hear	heard	heard
hide	hid	hidden
hit	hit	hit
hold	held	held
hurt	hurt	hurt
keep	kept	kept
know	knew	known
lay	laid	laid
lead	led	led
learn	learnt (learned)	learnt (learned)
leave	left	left
lend	lent	lent
let	let	let

Infinitive	Past	Past Participle
lie	lay	lain
light	lit	lit
lose	lost	lost
make	made	made
mean	meant	meant
meet	met	met
pay	paid	paid
put	put	put
read /ri:d/	read /red/	read /red/
ride	rode	ridden
ring	rang	rung
rise	rose	risen
run	ran	run
say	said	said
see	saw	seen
seek	sought	sought
sell	sold	sold
send	sent	sent
set	set	set
sew	sewed	sewn (sewed)
shake	shook	shaken
shine	shone	shone
shoot	shot	shot
show	showed	shown
shut	shut	shut
sing	sang	sung
sit	sat	sat
sleep	slept	slept
smell	smelt (smelled)	smelt (smelled)
speak	spoke	spoken
spell	spelt (spelled)	spelt (spelled)
spend	spent	spent
split	split	split
spread	spread	spread
spring	sprang	sprung
stand	stood	stood
steal	stole	stolen
stick	stuck	stuck
sting	stung	stung
stink	stank	stunk
strike	struck	struck
swear	swore	sworn
sweep	swept	swept
swim	swam	swum
take	took	taken
teach	taught	taught
tear	tore	torn
tell	told	told
think	thought	thought
throw	threw	thrown
understand	understood	understood
wake	woke	woken
wear	wore	worn
win	won	won
write	wrote	written

WORD LIST

Unit 1

actor
actress
age
Ankara
Argentina
artist
astronaut
be from
Beijing
boarding-school
Brazil
by the way
call
Canada
capital
cardinal number(s)
cathedral
China
college
country
dancer
doctor
Dublin
Edinburgh
Egypt
engineer
England
exactly
Excuse me
farmer
favourite
Finland
football
foreign
France
friend
Glasgow
great
Greece
History
Holland
Hungary
India
information
introduce
Ireland
issue
Italy
Japan
job
magazine
married
Maths
Mexico

Moscow
musician
nationality
neighbour
new
New Delhi
nice
Nice to meet you
ordinal number(s)
origin
page
people
pilot
please
Pleased to meet you
Poland
postman
reader
responsible for
Russia
Scotland
Spain
sport
student
the USA
too
Turkey
vet
waiter
Warsaw

Unit 2

ability
advertisement
all right
Arab
area
be missing
beard
big
brown
build
Bye
card
central
certainly
cheek
chin
club
complexion
computer games
cook
curly
dancing
dark

Denmark
describe
double
each
ear
eye
fair
fast
fat
flattish
Florence
full
greeting
guitar
hair
Have a nice evening
hear
hear from sb
height
helicopter
help sb up
here's
home address
hope
How are things?
join
last
later
Libya
light
like
lips
live
long
look like
love
madam
Mediterranean
middle-aged
most
motorbike
moustache
mouth
northern
Norway
nose
of course
old
pale
part
pen pal
pen-friend
phone number
plane
quite
rather

reading
request
right
Saudi Arabia
say goodbye
See you
sentence
short
sign
skiing
skin
slanting
slim
small
southern
speak
spell
straight
such as
Sweden
tall
teeth
thin
trumpet
type
usually
walk
wavy
well
well-built
wide
yellowish
young

Unit 3

a lot
also
armchair
attic
attractive
avenue
balcony
bargain
bath
bathroom
beautiful
bedroom
bedside cabinet
bedside table
behind
bench
block of flats
bookcase
Boston
brush

building
cabin
carpet
chair
chalet
cheap
child's bedroom
chimney
city centre
comfortable
cooker
cost
cupboard
curtain
cushion
desk
dining-room
dining table
dishwasher
door
double bed
downstairs
dressing table
estate agent
expensive
far from
farm
farmhouse
fireplace
first floor
flat
floor
flower
for rent
for sale
fridge
furniture
garage
garden
grass roof
great
ground floor
half
Home sweet home
houseboat
huge
inside
key
kitchen
lamp
lane
large
let me see
let's go
living-room
location

lovely
made of
main
mile
mirror
modern
month
mountain
mud hut
near
Nigeria
only
outside
per month
perfect
picture
pillow
plant
pleasant
plural
poster
pretty
price
quiet
rent
right now
river
road
roof
room
rug
shop
shower
single bed
singular
sink
size
sofa
sounds
spacious
stairs
street
study
swimming-pool
Switzerland
table
take (sb somewhere)
time
toilet
towel
upstairs
vase
view
village
wall
wardrobe

washbasin
window
wonderful
wood

Story 1 - Episode 1

accident
after
Be careful
boat
Don't be afraid!
Don't stand up!
Don't worry!
editor
episode
Help!
hire
I'm cold
instructions
It's gone
look for
maybe
monster
newspaper
office
order
photograph
Put ... on
quick
really
reporter
show
Sit down!
story
Take my hand
today
work for

Unit 4

a bit
actually
aged
appearance
ask
aunt
Best wishes
bicycle
bossy
brother
camp
character
cinema
classical music
clean

clever
conclusion
cousin
daughter
do the ironing
early
enjoy
every
exercise
family
family tree
father
finish
fish
fly
free time
full name
get up
give
go fishing
go on a picnic
go shopping
good-looking
gorgeous
grandfather
grandmother
grandparents
group
hate
hospital
husband
identify
introduction
kind
late
lazy
letter
listen to
local
main body
maniac
meet
member
minute
mother
nephew
next to
niece
not bad
occupation
open
parents
park
passport
patient
primary school

relatives
rock music
rude
shoes
sister
son
start
surgeon
T-shirt
That's all about me
theatre
though
travel
uncle
wash
watch
wife
work at
write back

Unit 5

always
angry
animal
aquarium
around the clock
arrival
arrive at
ask for more
at the moment
be afraid (of sth)
because
bird
bored
boring
breakfast
catch the train
chemist
clock face
close
club
countryside
cover evenings
customer
day
departure
diner
do the washing-up
dolphin trainer
during
early bird
feed
feel
field
generally

get dressed
go climbing
go dancing
go for long walks
go jogging
go windsurfing
guest
gym
happy
have a break
have a shower
have lessons
Holland
late-night shopping
life
lunch-time
man
milk the cows
museum
never
night
night owl
often
open air
open late
opening hours
owl
party
picnic
playing-field
post office
practise
rarely
relax
restaurant
satisfied
shark trainer
singer
sleep
sometimes
sorry
special
stressed
studio
tell the time
tense
the Dutch
tired
tiring
train
typical
village team
was born
weekend
work long hours

Unit 6

Africa
America
Antarctica
Australia
baby
body
butterfly
cage
carrot
chimpanzee
cold
collie
deer
distance
easily
eastern
eucalyptus
farm animal
feather
feet
female
fin
forest
friendly
front
fruit
funny
fur
group
hunt
ice
India
insect
intelligent
jump
lay eggs
learn
leaves
leg
lettuce
male
mammal
mane
mouse - mice
noise
other
Pacific Ocean
person
plain
pouch
reptile
rooster
sea lion
sharp claws

sheep
skin
smile
stripe
tail
thick
trunk
unusual
vegetable
warm sea
weigh
whisker
wild animal
wing
world

Story 1 - Episode 2

accident
afraid
amazing
castle
deep
envelope
interesting
mile
neck
safe
save
Scottish Highlands
surprised
tourist
unfortunately
upset
wrong

Unit 7

appear
autumn
beach
blow
boot
cap
Christmas tree
climate
cloudy
coat
decorate
dress
drive a car
foggy
freezing cold
glove
habit
Happy New Year

hat
heavy
hot
imagine
jacket
keep warm
make a snowman
miss
pick flowers
pyjamas
rainy
ride a horse
sandcastle
season
Season's greetings
shine
snow heavily
snowy
spring
summer
sunbathe
sunny
sunshade
swimming costume
temperature
throw snowballs
tie
tight
try on
warm
wear
weather
weather chart
windy
winter

Unit 8

bill
book a table
bottle
bowl
breakfast
busy
carton
cereal
cup
cut
delicious
dessert
dinner
dinner party
dish
drink
eat
food

forget
fork
frying-pan
glass
grilled
hand
helpful
home-made
how many
how much
hungry
instead
juice
knife
leave
light meal
loaf
lunch
meat
miss the chance
moment
occasion
order
packet
pepper steak
pick up
piece of
plate
polite
popular
recommendation
rice
rich sauce
roast chicken
serve
service
shopping list
slice
smoked fish
snack
something else
spoon
stall
strong coffee
superb
sweet
tasty
tea
thirsty
this way
tough
traditional

Unit 9

airport

ancient
bank
best friend
between
brick
bus stop
by bus
clothes
coast
corner
cottage
department store
difficult
doll
donkey
easy
electricity
ferry
few
film
fire escape
fire station
fishing boat
football match
game
get around
give directions
guest house
hard
hospital
in fact
in front of
island
it seems
left
money
narrow
noisy
nowadays
on
on foot
opposite
outside wall
pet
place
police station
port
public baths
reach
right
running water
school
souvenir shop
sports centre
state
stone

straight down
supermarket
take the first turning
toy
train station
warehouse
west
years ago

Story 2 - Episode 1

calm down
canoe
catch
destruction
die
drown
drum
expedition
head
hit
jungle
kill
nervous
paddle
prediction
rainforest
reception desk
save
watch
waterfall

Unit 10

achievement
admire
album
all-boy band
audition
ball
bassoon
biography
Cavalier
chemistry
complete
compose
concerto
continue
discover
divorce
Earl
education
event
fairy tale
famous for sth
fan

flute
for short
gold record
haircut
height of sb's career
important
in need
kindness
laughing
leukaemia
marriage
mathematics
medicine
nanny
Nobel Prize
nurse
opera
owner
penicillin
perform
physics
poor
popular
president
priest
professor
radium
receive
record company
role
scientist
sick
talented
tragic
wedding
world war

Unit 11

all night long
bark
beep
blind
bouquet
brave
break-in
bridge
bright
burst
canal
chase
competition
cries
desperately
dike
Emergency services

fall
flood
flow
for a while
frighten
get bigger and bigger
gold cup
heavy rain
hill
hold on
hole
horn
horrible experience
immediately
jeep
jump out
ladder
link
lock
lucky to be alive
mend
message
metal
nervously
notice
on sb's way home
panic
park ranger
point
rabbit
report
require
roar loudly
rush
Safari Park
save
scream
several
shocking
silk dress
strange
the Netherlands
tractor
tunnel
walk by
winner

Unit 12

accommodation
afford
birthplace
brochure
canal boat
celebrity
chain

Chile
convenient
desert
designer
drink
entertainment
exciting
fascinating
fashionable
film star
footprint
gift
handprint
heavy traffic
however
ideal
Luxembourg
main road
memorable
Mexican
moon
nightclub
nightlife
open-air
open-topped double-decker bus
pack with
peaceful
peacefulness
popular with
probably
pub
romantic
sightseeing
square
staff
star
street performer
the State of the Vatican City
three-star hotel
unforgettable
various
visitor
Wales

Story 2 - Episode 2

alligator
as a result
Atlantic Ocean
bag
chief
confuse
cut down
dead

destroy
disappear
disappointed
environment
expedition
fall down
follow sb
forever
hurt
land
lies at the mouth
mountain range
nearly
plant life
protect
river banks
run between
scary
serious
snapshot
There is no need
whole

Unit 13

accept
Aquarius
argue with
Aries
ballet lessons
breathe
Cancer
Capricorn
computer course
earn
event
evidence
extra money
fabulous
fire brigade
flying cars
food pills
for the rest of
garden party
Gemini
good news
have fun
health
health problems
honest
horrible
invitation
journey
Leo
Libra
lose money

Word List

lose weight
lucky
oxygen mask
perhaps
Pisces
plan
pollution
raincoat
Sagittarius
Scorpio
short journey
star sign
Taurus
trip
try
underwater cities
vehicle
Virgo
weather chart
welcome to

Unit 14

aerosol
alone
aluminium
appointment
aspirin
bad for
blow your nose
can
cheat in tests
chew gum
chopstick
classroom
cough syrup
create
danger
dentist
enter
factory
fight
fit and healthy
fizzy drink
flu
forbidden
full stomach
head for
headache
house rules
in public
it's your turn
jumper
keep in mind
kiss
leaflet

light fires
lodger
loud music
mouth
nearest
obligation
on time
optician
pack
park
permission
plastic
point
pollute
pre-packaged food
prohibition
public transport
push into
queue
recycling bin
refuse
regular exercise
remember
rent
rubbish
rubbish bin
sign
slipper
smell
smoking
sore throat
suncream
sunglasses
sweet
take your shoes off
tell jokes
the environment
throw
tip
toe
toothache
tram
tree
upward
useful
wash the dishes
washing-up liquid
What's the matter?

Unit 15

accidentally
already
Arc de Triomphe
awful
bazaar

bellboy
boat trip
call
camel
centre
Chinese
couscous
disgusting
dream
Egyptian
exhibit
experience
falafel
Fancy meeting you here
find
flea market
generously
handmade
heating
holiday destination
idea
in the middle of
just
magnificent
mask
nightmare
Notre Dame
opera
paella
painting
Pharaoh
pyramid
receptionist
reservation
return
ride
Sounds nice
spare key
Sphinx
state room
statue
stop working
suitcase
surprise
take a break
temple
the Seine
ticket
tip
tonight
travel agent
wallet
waste my time
worst
yet

Story 3 - Episode 1

bonnet
bright
bumper
can't stand
cry
dry
explanation
flashing lights
headlight
land
light
logical
rear-view mirror
research
seat
sky
slow down
spaceship
steering wheel
UFO
What on earth
wheel
windscreen
wing mirror

Story 3 - Episode 2

aboriginal
alien
automatic
believe
camera
certain
contact
develop
erase
happen
hot air balloon
human
memory
mention
metal box
primitive
raft
robe
similar
strange
study
technology
transport
understand

PHOTO FILE SECTION

UNIT 1

put your
photo
here

....

....

....

....

....

....

....

....

....

....

....

....

....

....

Amy

Eric   Frank

Max

Yoko   Lee

Lester

Dear Vicky,

I am in my new flat, at last! It's on the seventh floor of a big ..block of...

..*flats*... near the city centre. The flat is wonderful. It's got two bedrooms, a kitchen, a

.... and a huge living-room with a .... in it.

My favourite room is my bedroom, because it's very pretty. It's got a blue carpet on

the floor and a large .... with a great view of the city.

My comfortable .... is right next to the ....

There is also a small table in the room with a telephone and a .... on it.

I've got a big ...., a large wardrobe, a TV and a CD player in my

bedroom. I've also got some .... on the walls. My bedroom

has got a balcony, too. There are some .... on it.

Well, that's all for now. Come and see my new flat soon!

Love,

Paula

FOR RENT

BARGAIN!

FOR RENT

AROUND THE CLOCK WITH

Annie Franklin

People in Britain usually have toast with .... for breakfast, or

.... with milk. They drink instant coffee or

.... with milk. Sometimes, they have a traditional English breakfast. This includes

..........................., ..., ...,

.... and some slices of toast. Lunch is a quick meal because most

people are at work. They have a one-hour lunch break some time between 12 and 2pm. They

usually have a light meal, such as a ...., a ....

or a piece of .... Dinner is the main meal of the day. Most British

people have dinner early, between 6 and 8pm. A traditional full dinner is ....

or ...., meat with ...., and dessert —

.... or cheese — but nowadays not many British people have such a

big dinner. Sometimes they buy fish and .... or Chinese food from

take-away restaurants instead. On Sundays, they usually have a traditional Sunday lunch. This

is roast meat, such as .... or beef, with vegetables and

roast ....

The Blue Lagoon

The Blue Lagoon is the ....
....
....

The food is ....
....
....
....
....
....

A meal for two ....
....

The Blue Lagoon is a ....
.... Don't miss the chance to try its various dishes, but remember to book a table first
(Tel.: 6620102). Enjoy your meal.

Sammy the Wonder Horse

- warm summer day/Sally/ sit/under/big tree/next to/ house

- she/want/write/story/ for/competition/in/ school magazine

- Suddenly/Sally/hear her horse/make/strange noise

- Mr Thomas/her teacher/ give/her/first prize/for/story competition

- Sally/feel/really happy/ to be/winner

ACCOMMODATION:	Rosier - expensive, but very luxurious hotel / Hilton - biggest hotel in the city centre
PLACES TO VISIT:	the Brabo Fountain - take photographs the Cathedral - see paintings by Paul Rubens The National Maritime Museum - learn about the history of Antwerp Antwerp Zoo - one of the biggest in Europe
EATING OUT:	Maritime - excellent seafood restaurant Sir Anthony Van Dijck - restaurant with delicious traditional French-Belgian cuisine
SHOPPING:	Meir - main shopping street with lots of boutiques and Belgian chocolate shops the diamond quarter - buy or look at the beautiful diamonds
NIGHTLIFE:	bars and cafés - listen to live jazz music De Singel - see an opera

ANTWERP

This beautiful city in northern Belgium
has diamonds, beautiful buildings and lots more.

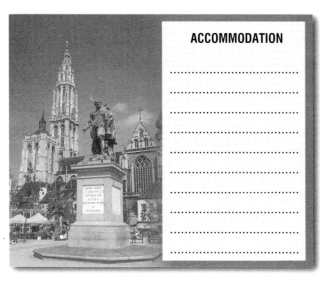

ACCOMMODATION

....
....
....
....
....
....
....
....
....
....

PLACES TO VISIT

....
....
....
....
....
....
....
....
....
....

EATING OUT ....
....
....
....

SHOPPING ....
....
....
....

NIGHTLIFE ....
....
....
....

Antwerp has so much
to offer — it's beautiful,
it's interesting and there
is always something to
do there. For a great
holiday in a northern
European city, try
Antwerp.

KEY

1 difficult / horrible week

2 exciting / pleasant / good week

3 receive a letter/letters

4 get an invitation

5 go on a short trip

6 have fun

7 have problems with your health

8 meet an interesting person

9 argue with someone

10 get a lot of money

12, Apple Street
Plymouth
PL7 6TQ
6 May, ...

Dear Steve,

Thank you for your letter. I am happy to hear that you want to change your bad habits.

There are a lot of things you can do to keep fit and healthy.

Firstly, you .... You

.... or ....

They aren't healthy at all. It's ....

and .... for breakfast. They will give you a good start to the day.

You .... or .... because

they are full of sugar. Why .... instead?

Also, it ....

or .... You will only get fat.

You .... Why don't you leave

the car at home and .... to work?

I hope my advice will help you. Good luck!

Love,

Aunt Claire

Culture
Clips

1 Routes to Central Europe

You don't have to fly to get from Britain to central Europe. Why not cross the English Channel by boat, or go through the Channel **Tunnel**?

Pre-reading Activity

1 **Look at the pictures and the map. Which of the following are true statements? Write T (true) or F (false).**

1 Dover is in Belgium. ....
2 Folkestone is in the south of England. ....
3 The Channel Tunnel goes under the seabed. ....

Reading

2 **a) Read the texts and tick (✓) the correct box for the statements 1-6. Then explain the words in bold.**

	Right	Wrong	Doesn't Say
1 It takes 35 minutes to travel from Dover to Calais by ferry.	☐	☐	☐
2 A Seacat is a high-speed catamaran.	☐	☐	☐
3 The Channel Tunnel is 50km below the seabed.	☐	☐	☐
4 The most popular way to cross the Channel is by Seacat.	☐	☐	☐
5 The Channel Tunnel opened in 1995.	☐	☐	☐
6 Ostend is in Belgium.	☐	☐	☐

Dover, on the south coast of England, is one of the world's busiest **ports**. Every day lots of **ferries** and high-speed catamarans called 'Seacats' arrive and leave. It's a short trip across the English Channel to Calais and Dunkirk in France, or to Ostend and Zeebrugge in Belgium. A traditional ferry takes 90 minutes from Dover to Calais, but a catamaran is much faster and can make the same journey in 35 minutes.

b) Match the highlighted words to their opposites in the list.
- boring • long • different • modern
- slower

England

London

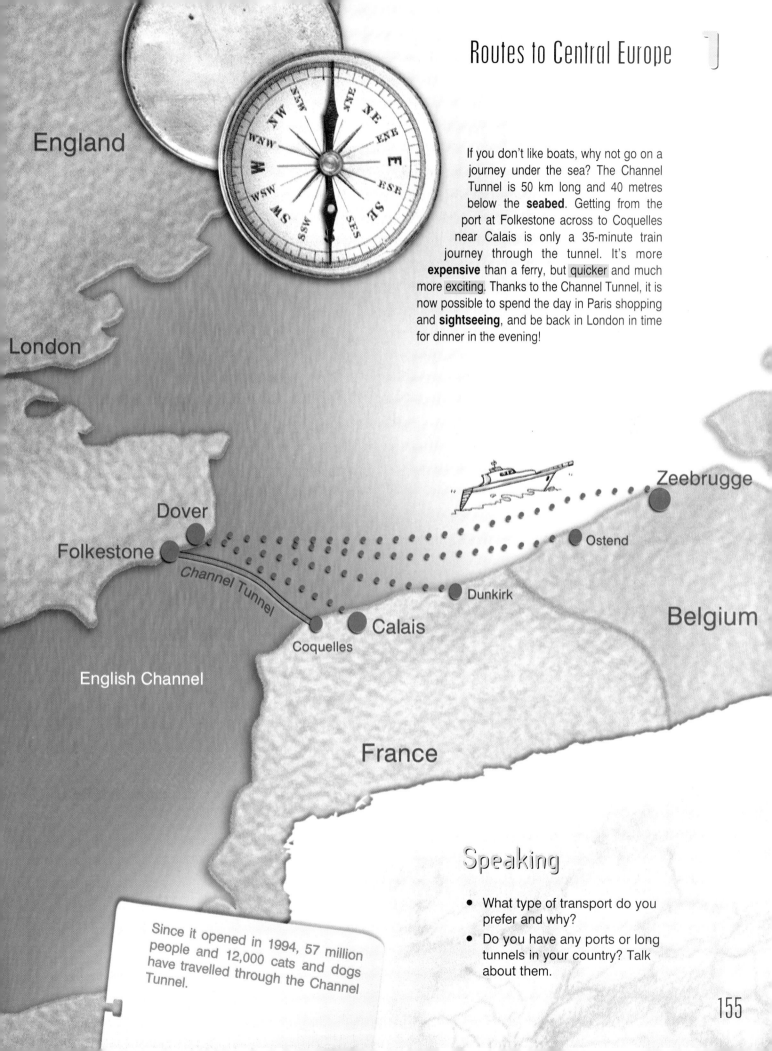

If you don't like boats, why not go on a journey under the sea? The Channel Tunnel is 50 km long and 40 metres below the **seabed**. Getting from the port at Folkestone across to Coquelles near Calais is only a 35-minute train journey through the tunnel. It's more **expensive** than a ferry, but quicker and much more exciting. Thanks to the Channel Tunnel, it is now possible to spend the day in Paris shopping and **sightseeing**, and be back in London in time for dinner in the evening!

Zeebrugge

Dover

Ostend

Folkestone

Channel Tunnel

Dunkirk

Belgium

Coquelles

Calais

English Channel

France

Since it opened in 1994, 57 million people and 12,000 cats and dogs have travelled through the Channel Tunnel.

Speaking

- What type of transport do you prefer and why?
- Do you have any ports or long tunnels in your country? Talk about them.

2 Canadian Cities

Pre-reading Activity

1 **Look at the pictures (A-E). Which shows ...**
- a Chinese pagoda?
- a totem pole?
- a café?
- a military parade?
- an art gallery and gardens?

2 **Look at the map and point to:**
- Vancouver • Montreal • Ottawa

3 **Which one is in the south-west of Canada?**
Which two are in the south-east of Canada?

Reading

4 **a) Read the texts and mark the statements T (true) or F (false). Then explain the words in bold.**

1 Vancouver is the capital of Canada. ....
2 Canada Place is a large park. ....
3 The Chinese Garden is in Montreal. ....
4 People in Ottawa speak French and English. ....
5 Ottawa has over 60 annual festivals. ....

b) Match the highlighted words to their opposites in the list.
- dirty • plain • new • small • ugly

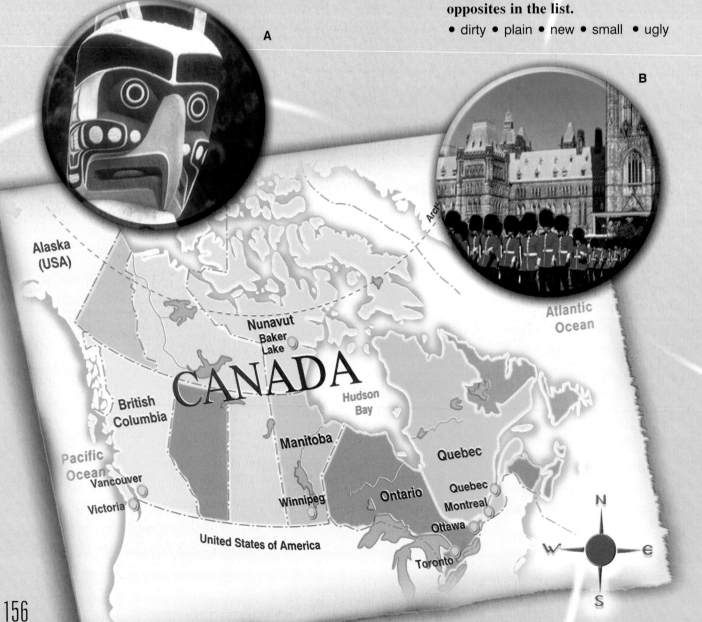

A

B

Alaska (USA)

Nunavut
Baker Lake

CANADA

British Columbia

Pacific Ocean
Vancouver

Victoria

Manitoba

Winnipeg

Hudson Bay

Ontario

Quebec

Quebec

Montreal

Ottawa

Atlantic Ocean

Toronto

United States of America

N
W E
S

156

Vancouver

Vancouver is one of the most beautiful places in Canada. It has clean streets and green parks and great views of the Pacific Ocean, to the west and huge mountains to the east. Vancouver is an **ideal** city. One of its main **attractions** is Stanley Park, where there are **sandy** beaches, lakes, and even Indian **totem poles**. You must also visit Canada Place. It has a **conference centre** a luxury hotel, a huge cinema and there are special events held there all year round.

C

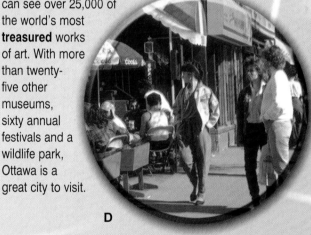

E

Ottawa

Ottawa, the capital city of Canada, is a wonderful **mixture** of old and new buildings. This green city is a **cultural** and historical centre for Canada. The people are friendly and speak both French and English. Parliament Hill is a popular tourist **spot** where visitors can watch **military parades**. Ottawa is also the **home** of Canada's National Gallery. It is **surrounded** by beautiful gardens. Inside, visitors can see over 25,000 of the world's most **treasured** works of art. With more than twenty-five other museums, sixty annual festivals and a wildlife park, Ottawa is a great city to visit.

D

Montreal

The city of Montreal is sometimes called the Paris of North America. Two thirds of the people speak French. The area of Old Montreal is very **popular** with tourists because of its **narrow** streets, old buildings and European-style cafés and restaurants. In the Botanical Gardens there are over 22,000 types of **plants** and flowers from all over the world. The Chinese Garden is beautiful and it has a huge colourful pagoda.

Speaking

- Which of these cities would you like to visit, and why?
- Name three cities in your country.

  Which one is your favourite?
  What do you like about it?
  What can you see and do there?

3 Teatime

Pre-reading Activity

1 Look at the pictures (A-F). Which shows ...
- cake?
- kippers?
- a sandwich?
- a pot of tea?
- biscuits?
- toast?

Reading

2 **a)** Read the texts and answer the questions (1-5), then explain the words in bold.

b) Read the texts again and find words which are similar in your mother tongue.

c) Can you put the steps in the correct order?

How to make a good cup of tea:

A ☐ let it **brew** for about 5 minutes

B ☐ warm the **teapot** (using hot water)

C ☐ drink and enjoy!

D ☐ put one **teabag** per person into the teapot, plus an extra one 'for the pot' and add boiling water

E ☐ **pour** into cups and add milk and sugar

F ☐ put the kettle on to boil

1 How many cups of tea do the British drink every day?

2 What do people have for high tea?

3 What time is 'elevenses'?

4 Where is Earl Grey tea from?

5 When do people drink fruit tea?

Everybody knows that the British drink tea, but did you know that they drink around 165 **million** cups every day? Tea is not just a drink, it is a tradition, and is **part** of the history and **culture** of the UK.

Afternoon tea is a **popular** tradition that started in the early 1800s when people had tea parties in their homes or went out to tea shops or tea rooms at around 4 o'clock in the afternoon. Today, people continue this tradition and tea is served with a light meal of sandwiches, biscuits, cream cakes or fruit cake. In some parts of Britain, afternoon tea is called high tea and usually **includes** a hot dish. It is **similar** to a cooked breakfast, and foods such as kippers or eggs with toast as well as cold meats are served.

Tea breaks are another tradition that have become a part of daily life. In the past, when workers began their day at about 6am, they took a break in the morning at around 11am to drink tea and have a light **snack**. Today many people call this 'elevenses' and have a cup of tea and a biscuit.

Nowadays, a wide **variety** of different teas are available and different blends are drunk at different times. English breakfast tea is taken in the morning because it has a strong **flavour** and it wakes you up ready for the day. Darjeeling from India and Earl Grey from China are **mild** and are best drunk with afternoon tea. Herbal and fruit teas are popular and are drunk at any time of the day.

Speaking

- Do people in your country drink tea or coffee? What is your national drink?
- Do you have any unusual meals like high tea?

A

B

C

D

E

F

4 East Meets West

Pre-reading Activity

1 a) Which places do you think these articles are about?

b) Look at the pictures (A-F). Which shows ...
- a dragon carving?
- a Chinese lion dance?
- firecrackers?
- a Chinese Gate?
- a Chinese dish?
- Chinese lanterns?

Reading

2 a) Read the texts and mark the statements NY (New York) or L (London). Then explain the words in bold.

1 Chinatown is on the east side of Manhattan. ....
2 Shopkeepers give the lion dancers money. ....
3 No cars are allowed. ....
4 At New Year you can hear the sound of firecrackers. ....
5 It has the largest Chinese community outside of Asia. ....

b) Read the texts again and underline the sentences/phrases which best match each picture.

c) Use your dictionary to explain the words in bold.

d) Suggest synonyms for the highlighted words.

A

Did you know that there are more Chinese people living in the United States than in any other country outside of Asia? Or that America's largest Chinese community is **based** in New York City's very own Chinatown? Any visitor to Manhattan's east side will feel as if they are in another world. It's a huge area with hundreds of Chinese restaurants where you can try delicious **oriental** dishes. Visitors enjoy walking along the **winding** streets full of colourful shops decorated with oriental carvings and images. There are also fruit, vegetable, meat and fish markets, selling everything you need to make your own Chinese meal.

New York City's Chinatown really **comes to life** during the Chinese New Year celebrations. The streets are **crowded** with people of all nationalities watching the amazing dragon and lion dances and admiring the **incredible** costumes. Traditionally, Chinese shopkeepers must pay the lion dancers so that their shop has a good year. The more money they pay, the more luck they will have.

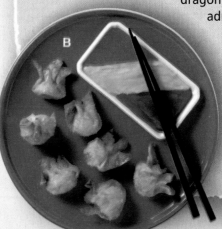

B

Speaking

- What are the main nationalities of the people living in your country?
- What other nationalities live in your country? How do they live?
- How do you celebrate New Year?

London's Chinatown is in the Gerrard Street area in the city centre. The Chinese Gate, which is a beautiful oriental entrance to Chinatown, is green and red and people see it as a **symbol** of the success of the area. There is also a pavilion and no cars are allowed in the area. The streets are full of Chinese restaurants, food stores and specialist shops. Although it is called Chinatown, these **businesses** are from all over the Far East, including Thailand, Indonesia, Japan and Hong Kong. The area has become a **major** tourist attraction and part of London's culture.

Britain's Chinese community celebrate Chinese New Year in style. London's Chinatown is **decorated** with lanterns and flags and the sound of noisy firecrackers fills the air. The whole area becomes a huge market with **stalls** selling everything from cheap souvernirs to **antique** Chinese vases. As in New York and all over the world, the lion dance is the main feature of the celebration. However, there are many other special Chinese traditions. For example, children receive gifts of money in red packets with symbols on them to bring good luck.

5 Festive Fun

Pre-reading Activity

1 Look at the pictures. How are they related to the title? Which shows:
- The Lord Mayor in a gold coach?
- a firework display?
- a maypole dance?
- a yachting event?
- a May Queen?

Reading

2 **a)** Read the texts and answer the questions (1-6). Write (L) for the Lord Mayor's Show, (M) for May Festivals and (C) for Cowes Week. Then explain the words in bold.

1 You can watch the event from special boats.
2 Crowds blow whistles and wave Union Jacks. ......
3 People use flowers as decorations. ......
4 People perform special dances. ......
5 There is a firework display. ......
6 There are horses in the procession. ......

b) Read the texts again. Are there any words similar to words in your language?

c) Match the highlighted words to their synonyms.
- show • welcoming • beautiful • fantastic
- ideal • customs

The Lord Mayor's Show

The Lord Mayor's Show is a colourful London tradition which started in 1215 and takes place every November. The Lord **Mayor** is the person who makes important **decisions** about the city.

During the show he travels through central London in a gold coach at the front of a large **parade**. There are soldiers, marching bands, horses and brightly-coloured floats in the parade. People wear beautiful **costumes** and follow the coach as they listen to the **bands** playing.

The whole **procession** is nearly four kilometres long. It is the largest parade of its kind in the world. The streets are full of people who come to watch and **cheer** just as they did when the famous Dick Whittington was Lord Mayor in 1397. Nowadays, the crowds **blow whistles** and wave **Union Jack** flags. At the end of the parade there is a spectacular firework display.

Cowes Week

May Festivals

1st May is called May Day in Britain and there are lots of different traditions and festivals to **celebrate** the first day of spring.

In many English towns and villages the local people dance around a maypole which is decorated with flowers and **ribbons**. They also choose a pretty young girl to be the May Queen. She then **leads** a parade around the streets and Morris Dancers wear flowers and bells and perform a special dance.

In Padstow in Cornwall, the May Day celebrations include the Hobby Horse Festival. Two men wear costumes and **masks** and go around the town followed by dancers and musicians.

Well dressing is another May Day tradition. Villagers decorate the drinking wells with pictures made from **clay** and flowers and people come from far away to admire them.

The Isle of Wight is a small island on the south coast of England. The sea around the island is perfect for **sailing**. Perhaps that's why the small port of Cowes has become one of the most important centres for yachting in the world.

The **highlight** of the year is Cowes Week, which takes place in early August and **dates back** to 1826. More than 1,000 boats come to Cowes for the many different **races**. Thousands of people watch from the port or from one of the hundreds of **spectator** boats. After each day's sailing, there are lots of yacht club parties, balls and **public** events. On the last day there is a huge firework display. Members of the royal family come to visit and everybody has a great time on this friendly and beautiful island.

Calendar of Events

Here are some more important UK festivals and events:

January	Burns Night
February	Pancake Day
March	Mother's Day
April	April Fool's Day
May	Brighton Arts Festival
June	Royal Ascot Races
July	Henley Royal Regatta
August	Notting Hill Carnival
September	Braemer Royal Highland Gathering
October	Halloween
November	Bonfire Night
December	New Year's Eve

Speaking

- Which festival interests you most?
- Choose one of the pictures and describe it, then talk about the festival.
- Do you have any interesting festivals in your country? Talk about them.
- Make a Calendar of Events for your country, then choose two or three events and describe them.

American English - British English Guide

Cars and Driving

American English	British English
antenna	aerial
circle, rotary	roundabout
defroster	window heater
detour	diversion
divided highway	dual carriageway
fender	wing
flat (tire)	flat tyre, puncture
gas, gasoline	petrol
gas station	petrol station, garage
gear shift	gear lever, stick
high beams	full lights
hood	bonnet
intersection	crossroads
interstate, highway, freeway	motorway
low beams	lights dipped
minibus	van/minibus
motorcycle	motorbike, motorcycle
overpass	flyover
parking lot	car park
pass (vehicle, etc)	overtake, pass
pedestrian crossing	zebra crossing, pedestrian crossing
rental car	hire car
transmission	gear box
truck	lorry, van
turn signals	indicators
windshield	windscreen

Travelling/Commuting

American English	British English
airplane	aeroplane
baggage claim	baggage reclaim
bus	coach
cab	taxi
one-way (ticket)	single
railroad	railway
round trip (ticket)	return (ticket)
sidewalk	pavement
subway	underground, tube
underpass	subway

Food

American English	British English
appetizers	starters
baked potato	jacket potato
broil	grill
candy	sweets
candy store	confectioner, sweet shop
canned	tinned
cookie	biscuit
corn	sweetcorn, maize
cotton candy	candy floss
dessert	pudding, sweet, dessert
eggplant	aubergine
fish sticks	fish fingers
French fries	chips
ground meat	mince
jello	jelly
jelly	jam
oatmeal	porridge
potato chips	crisps
preserves	conserves
without or with (milk/cream in coffee)	black or white
zucchini	courgettes

Others

American English	British English
account	bill, account
any place, anywhere	anywhere
apartment	flat
area code	dialling code (phone)
attorney, lawyer	solicitor
backpack	rucksack
band aid	sticking plaster
bathrobe	dressing gown
bathtub	bath
bill (currency)	banknote
billion = thousand million	billion = million million
blind (n)	hide (n)
botanical garden	botanic garden
bureau	chest of drawers
busy (telephone)	engaged
call, phone	ring up, phone, call
cheap (badly made/ done)	shoddy
check (restaurant)	bill

American English	British English	American English	British English
clippings	cuttings	nothing, zero	nil
closet	cupboard	office (doctor's/dentist's)	surgery
closet (hanging clothes)	wardrobe	on line	on stream
connect (telephone)	put through	open house	open day
counter clockwise	anticlockwise	overalls	dungarees
crazy	mad	pacifier	dummy
crib (for a baby)	cot	pants, trousers	trousers
davenport, sofa, couch	sofa, settee, couch	pantyhose, nylons	tights
desk clerk	receptionist	parka	anorak
dish towel	tea towel	pocketbook	purse, wallet
down town	centre (city/business)	polo neck	roll neck, polo neck
drapes	curtains	pool (pocket billiards)	snooker
dresser	chest of drawers	principal	headmaster
druggist	chemist	public school	state school
drugstore, pharmacy	chemist's (shop)	purse	handbag
overalls	jeans, dungarees	rent (a car)	hire (a car)
duplex	semi-detached	reservations	bookings
elevator	lift	rest room	toilet, cloakroom, public convenience
equip, fit out	fit (v)		
eraser	rubber, eraser	run (for election)	stand (for election)
fall	autumn	sack lunch	packed lunch
faucet	tap	sales clerk, sales girl	shop assistant
fire (v) (from employment)	sack	schedule	timetable
		Scotch tape	Sellotape
first floor, second floor etc	ground floor, first floor etc	shopping cart	shopping trolley
flashlight	torch	shorts (underwear)	pants
freshman (at university)	1st year undergraduate	sick	ill
front desk	reception	sleep in	lie in
garbage, trash	rubbish	sneakers	trainers
garbage can, trash can	dustbin, bin	soccer	football
garters	suspenders	sports	sport
grade	class, form	stand in line	queue
intermission	interval	store, shop	shop
janitor	caretaker, porter	suspenders	braces
jump rope	skipping rope	telephone booth	telephone box
laundromat	laundrette	trash bag	bin liner
lay off (v)	make redundant	tricky	dodgy
layoff	redundancy	tuition (for schooling)	fee
line	queue	two weeks	fortnight, two weeks
lost and found	lost property	undershirt	vest
mail	post	vacation	holiday
mailman	postman	vacuum (n, v), vacuum cleaner (n)	hoover (n, v)
make a reservation	book		
math	maths	vest	waistcoat
movie	film	yard	garden
movie house/theater	cinema	z (pronounced "zee")	z (pronounced "zed")
news stand	newsagent	zero	nought, oh
non-profit-organization, not-for-profit	charity	zip code	post code

Grammar

American English	British English
He **just left**. / He **has just left**.	He **has just left**.
We **saw** that film.	We **have seen** that film.
Did he hand in the report **yet**?	**Has he handed** in the report **yet**?
Hello, is **this** David?	Hello, is **that** David?
Do you have a ticket? / **Have you got** a ticket?	**Have you got** a ticket?

Spelling

American English	British English
aluminum	aluminium
analyze	analyse
center	centre
check (n)	cheque (n)
color	colour
defense	defence
honor	honour
jewelry	jewellery
labor	labour
practice (n, v)	practice (n), practise (v)
program	programme
realize	realise
theater	theatre
tire	tyre
trave(l)ler	traveller

Expressions with prepositions and particles

American English	British English
different **from/than**	different **from/to**
live **on** X street	live **in** X street
on a team	**in** a team
on the weekend	**at** the weekend
Monday **through** Friday	Monday **to** Friday
be **in the** hospital	be **in** hospital
in the future	**in** future